Charles Livingstone

[Memoir]

Charles Livingstone

[Memoir]

ISBN/EAN: 9783743606401

Printed in Europe, USA, Canada, Australia, Japan

Cover: Foto ©ninafisch / pixelio.de

Manufactured and distributed by brebook publishing software (www.brebook.com)

Charles Livingstone

[Memoir]

in at once and not sleep in the

path for he is anxious to see the

There are small rapids near the mouth of the Chobe but the rest of the way the water is smooth

&c. Herds of cattle graze on

the islands, on ~~the~~ river. There are three varieties

of cattle a very small Batoka breed of

beautiful shape and remarkably tame; a large kind

~~with~~ many of which have pendant horns, loose at

the roots; and a still largest

beast to carry. The killed at morning the cattle pen ~~[illegible]~~ Always empties pit sloops ~~the [illegible] kind of bedding~~ had a refreshing draught of milk. ~~from~~

~~this~~

~~[illegible]~~ from a boy of 10 who had charge of the establishment, during his father's absence. according to

Matabele ideas the cattle pool is the proper school for them to be brought up in, here they receive a very ^the right sort of^ ~~sort~~ of ~~edu-~~ education: Strong Easterly winds blow daily from noon till midnight and continue till the October rains set in Whirlwinds resembling

[illegible] [illegible] nearly [illegible] [illegible] [illegible]
[illegible] [illegible] [illegible] the path
[illegible] [illegible] [illegible] [illegible] The
wind [illegible] [illegible] [illegible] [illegible]
all points of the compass; whirling
round and round [illegible] [illegible] eddies
it swept up hundreds of feet into
the air a cont[illegible] dense dark [illegible] that
cloud of the black pulverized
soil of the plains with the dried grass

and pokes with [illegible]

[illegible] . The [illegible]

[illegible] them [illegible] to the [illegible]

times and [illegible] them into the [illegible]

forms and [illegible] the [illegible]

~~[illegible]~~ [illegible]

[illegible] could [illegible]

[illegible] and might be [illegible]

the [illegible] ~~the [illegible]~~ and [illegible]

all the [illegible] and [illegible]

any visible letter spaces. The same

this time in a legal case is dealing

with a quiet man in a happy land

thought he be asleep, but he was in

the middle and they had quickly realised

There are but few of these remarks

between disaster and the father and

a great bark to ~~[illegible]~~ near a running

torrent, huts. A man hunted [illegible]

from this [illegible] ~~[illegible]~~ [illegible]

under a tree; A young [illegible]

with [illegible] large things [illegible]

hang, ~~xxxx~~ [illegible] to ~~[illegible]~~ receive [illegible]

from the chief who [illegible]

to the people [illegible] taken to the

Mokele

and conducted us to a house and a
bought a remarkably fine cow as a
present from the Chief. This was a
time of hunger here, and this was the
meat but a piece [illegible] from
the [illegible] valley. We remember

is classic beef. Let the "Acclimatisation Society" increase, multiply, the number of beeves and it will benefit humanity immensely more than it possibly could by the introduction of every wild animal, from ~~the~~ elephants down to ~~the~~ crockodile ~~alligator~~.

It must be confessed however that it is rather awkward to sit down to a meal of nothing else but [illegible] however excellent it may be. Even in the form of bread, potatoes, or vegetables to accompany it, and then is an unpleasant feeling of something wanting. But what do they have for Kitchen enquired a sympathetic Scotch woman of an Irish neighbour whose family flourished on potatoes, Oh they make the small potatoes Kitchen the large ones. We made the fat Kitchen the lean The Makololo eat all the fat first

afterwards eat the bean & cast off all the provi
on bread if they have any,

A Constant stream of visitors called on us the day after our arrival. Several who had been afflicted during the Drs absence seemed to be once happified on seeing him again. All were in low spirits, A severe drought had cut off the crops, and destroyed the pastures of Lingwaste and the people were ~~[illegible]~~ over the

brought troops of [illegible] in its [illegible]
Believing himself betrayed by [illegible] he
[illegible] a number of his Chief
Men and put some of them to death with
their families; others fled to distant
towns and are living in exile. The

Sinamane and Mnembe were independ-
and ~~Mashotlane~~ Moshotwane at the Falls, and
Sekeletu, are thereby virtually at defiance,
Sebituane's wise policy in treating the
conquered tribes along with his own Makololo
as all the children of the chief and
equally eligible to the highest honours
had been abandoned by his successors
married none but Makololo wives and

respecting the unseen Sekeletu
his fingers are found to have grown
like an eagle's talons, and his face
so frightfully distorted that no one
could recognize him. Some begin
to mind ~~them doubts~~ that he is really the
son of the great Sebituane, the founder
of the nation, slain in battle and.

"In the days of the great war (Sebituane)

said his only sister whose husband Sekeletu

had killed "~~There were~~ – We once had chiefs and

little chiefs and ~~other minor officers~~ elders

to carry on the government ~~of the tribe~~

and the Great Chief knew them all

given de hauts up. They cannot cure
him and pronounce the disease in-
-curable, and old doctor from a
distant tribe has come to see what
he can do for him and on his skill
he hangs his last hopes. She allows
no one to see him except his uncle,
and mother.
Making inclusive seclusion an essential
condition of the ~~[illegible]~~ medicine-pe[illegible] cure; he
fees [illegible] notwithstanding for the [illegible];

of his finger nails which was nothing

what ever in

remarkable, as all the Makololo

unaccountably finger

Gentlemen wear ~~very~~ long nails

he has the quiet unostentatious manner

& also distinctly

of his father, speaks slowly in a

low pleasant voice, and very distinct

-cept perhaps on the subject of his

having been bewitched, whom he

is ~~attending~~ here, he exhibits unmistakable

symptoms of being affected with the

witchcraft "monomania", "his

Aunt's husband had tried the bewitching medicine

first on her, and seeing that it succeeded

gave a stronger dose to him in the

flesh of a goat cooked and he has had the

disease ever since". He asked for

out of the hands of the physicians already
it being bad policy to under value any of the profession
employed, and ~~the being~~ anxious to go on
with her remedies "She said had not given
him up yet and wished to try for another
Month If by that time there was no cure
she would hand him over to the white

was one of the cases in which Medical
women are actuated by disinterested benev-
olence. ~~No woman could be better for~~
~~[illegible] [illegible] the consciousness of having~~ tried
~~to do a good deed.~~ ~~The disease~~
~~manifested itself chiefly in his legs,~~
arms
and face, ~~[illegible] [illegible] [illegible] by the~~ new

it with the astringent bark in powder, ~~tores~~ ~~practise in her country~~ of her country. She desisted from

on recovering a kind of something that

perhaps, the medicine of the white people as

the medicine of the blacks might not work

quince preserves along with the tea which

all the way
had been brought to him from Benguela

Makele
The headman of Dest. the, ~~[illegible]~~ and

Sebituane's sister were ordered to provide

us with food as Sekeletu was not

in Linyanti. We found a black

trader from the west coast purchasing

ivory, slaves & some yellow traders from the
were selling horses at 10 tusks each
South, ~~[illegible] after [illegible],~~

~~[illegible] traders from [illegible] paid~~

~~him a visit.~~ It is worthy of note

country from the Kapue to Sinamane,
than anywhere else in the country;
The next trader from [illegible] was taken,
in orders for goods for his next year's trip
Fashion is as despotic in Sesheke and
Linyanti as in London and Paris. The
ladies will not wear beads that are out of
fashion however pretty they may be,
The chief is a great horse fancier and
has invested, pretty largely in horse flesh, but

to purchased, A party was sent last
year, with money to the guild to purchase five horses
transported from Lisbon, all four died on the
passage, and the owners, then brought out
the five tails, and laid them before the
Sheikh, "A Portuguese at one of the
stopping stations had been like them
They, and him look at the horses, and
came to them, and was sure that he left the

~~[illegible]~~ He could not understand why all the horses the Chief bought should die; he thought they should endeavour to get a few bull mules, and cow mules, in order to raise a breed of mules which he had heard were tougher than horses.

The young men of the chief's body-guard a jolly set, have a new species of [illegible] ~~A fellow mounts~~ One mounts on the [illegible] but no bridle, {[illegible] both hands} and dashes off at full

four hours is kept at this work till
he is completely exhausted, each
of the Guards being anxious to show that
he can keep on the horse longer than
the others. Thus, taking one about
of [illegible] the first and [illegible] knocks
up the best horse, they [illegible]

~~The number of cereals, that fruit, or~~
~~vegetables or spice seems to be very~~
~~small.~~ ~~If we now consider these a,~~
food cultivated in this the
native ~~which the food~~ in the Atlantic
centre
of the Continent ~~we find little but~~
consists of Holcus sorghum -
Pennisetum - millets Maize -
~~Sorghum, Millet~~ Maize, Groundnuts,
ground nuts - under ground beans
- Beans - cucumbers - melons
~~and a pumpkin fruits. Maize and~~
pumpkins - Holcus saccharatum
sugar cane - cassava - bananas -
~~Rice and bananas~~ ~~Manioc or~~
sweet potatoes - tobacco - cotton
and hemp = ~~but~~ wheat, Rice &
~~Cassava, Sweet potatoes~~ and yams.

They have never seen, ~~in any kind~~
nor have they
Garden vegetables. ~~any of the kind~~

~~and a species of cucumber~~ They have

~~neither [illegible]~~
nor
Any of the fruit found near the [illegible]
such as mangoes, oranges &c
are which have been introduced to

Africa from other countries.

For the best food for the body and the

like England
most valuable for the country of Africa
must be
~~is~~ indebted to other parts of the world.

~~And will continue so to be for many~~

~~generations.~~ ~~It may be worthy~~

~~of~~ remark that they have both Cotton

quite equal
~~and sugar cane~~ in the interior, though

suffering from hunger. They have no
horses and game there cannot easily be
procured without; he shot meat for
them and was apprehensive that they
would hardly live to see the [illegible]

you had lived up this year and months

of longer to lead a [illegible] far more

than usually violent. Among

the [illegible] inhabitants of the place

Mr Helmann told the Chief that he did

not intend to remain there and wished

to go on to seek a more healthy locality,

the latter saying that the [illegible] appeared to

take him to [illegible] if he liked

[illegible]

that better, but while they were getting

Helmore was the first white person who fell

a victim to the Interior fatal Malaria [illegible]

The survivor missionary told the people

that although his wife had died, he

did not mean to leave them but would

remain and go on with the missionary

work. Notwithstanding the slander

came near this missionary work of preaching the gospel at once. When some young men at once learning a few of the hymn tunes, he taught them. All liked him and spoke kindly of him, and were sorry that he died. There is no doubt that in a short time he would have exerted a powerful and happy influence over the tribe, but he was cut down by fever in about

position. Four out of the nine Europeans

were dead and his own wife was lying

ill of the fever. His having been but a

short time in Africa his knowledge of

the native language was limited. He

accordingly took the wise course of

leaving the country, but his wife died

before he reached the healthy district.

The native servants ~~had never seen~~

~~Some of his natives thought fit the~~

the fever in their own country thought the

Makololo had poisoned the missionaries

~~and~~ to appear ~~to have~~ calculating that

But although the

~~our~~ former ~~ministry~~. ~~The~~ Makololo

not poison. There is no occasion

for suspecting poison. The fever is

poison enough. We have heard the

symptoms of the poison ~~he~~ as described
the summer

scores of times. They came from the

It was
~~Heart of the~~ African fever and nothing

else.

On hearing that there was a bare possibility, of steamers getting, as far as Sinamane, but never above the Grand Victoria Falls, he asked with charming simplicity if a Cannon could not blow away the Falls, so as to allow the vessel to come up to Sesheke. It was suggested that the best thing for him and his people would be to remove at once to the healthy highlands on the Kafue; he carefully

As they had come originally from the healthy South, this fever is unknown [rather] its ravages were as frightful among them as amongst Europeans on the coast. Sebituane's sister described its first appearance among the tribe after settling at Linyanti. Numbers of them were seized with a shivering, [between] and from till they died. About this year all

preferred the peace the highlands ~~[illegible]~~ they

were afraid ~~lying~~ ~~waste~~ to go there The multitude

would come and ~~steal~~ rob them of their cattle

Despite the Sultan with all his retinue

fighters could not in the last ~~[illegible]~~ that enemy [illegible] his young wife would make a ~~[illegible]~~ run

the Mission with, for the time the Makololo

They were as much afraid of the ~~Makololo~~ Matebele

as the black conquerors were of the

Makololo. but if the Dr & his wife

would come with them they would for

as they thought Mosilikatse would

not attack a place where the daughter

of his friend Moffat was living.

The Makololo are by far the most

we have met. None but brave & daring
men remain long with Sebituane
his stern discipline soon eradicates cowardi
Death was the inevitable ~~[illegible]~~ doom of the
coward. If the chief saw a man
running away from the fight he rushed
after him with amazing speed and cut
him down, or hurled till he retur

many manly virtues. They were
truthful and never stole except
what they considered the honourable
way, of lifting cattle or in fair fight
but this can hardly be said of their sons

vices peculiar to a menial and degraded race.
A few of the old Makololo cautioned us not
to leave any of our things exposed as the blacks
were great thieves. And some of our black
men advised us to be on our guard as the
Makololo would steal. The very few
trifling articles we lost were stolen by a
young Makololo who on being spoken to on
the subject showed great ingenuity in excusing
himself by a most plausible [illegible] into the
The old Makololo were hard workers and did not consider
labour as beneath them but their sons, never worth regard,
[illegible] others as fit only for being [illegible] of black servants.
The Makololo however are
Sekeletu's [illegible] than the river tribes, had the advantage over him in
knowing how to manage canoes had his warriors taught how
to manage canoes but my [illegible] black carry paddle &
readily superior to all the [illegible] clear,
all their dishes baskets stools & canoes are made by the
black tribes. Houses built by women & black servants.

and would be considered as beautiful any

the Portuguese of either. They are lighter

in colour; Manners pleasant (Continuance

and are remarkably quiet of appearance

They dress neatly, having a Kilt and

Mantle, and many ornaments.

Sebituane's sister, the head Lady of Sesheke

wore 18 solid brass rings, as thick as

one finger on each leg and three of

copper under each knee; 19 brass

The wealthy old men who have plenty

of cattle marry [illegible] of the prettiest

the

young-girls. An ugly old fellow who

was so blind that a servant had to lead

run along the path heedless of the
very handsomest young man in the
whole town, One of them, the daughter
of a hotel keeper, at least half a
century younger than himself
"Do you like him?" She was asked
Not so replied I told him [illegible]

uncertainty
importance is, leads to a good deal of immorality,

Wives are not bought and sold among
~~though the~~ marriage ~~in the case~~ looks like a bargain
the Matabele, ~~in some countries, it~~

~~thought so~~ The husband hands over to
in-law
the ~~father~~ father, a certain number

of cows, not as purchase money for the

bride but to purchase the right to

45 The parents make a sacrifice in parting with their child, and the husband must sacrifice some of his property to heal the breach made in theirs. When she dies, the husband gives one ot[her] again to cause entire severance or give her up

but not of her children

The Hotel ladies [illegible] the soft ~~[illegible]~~ small delicate hands and feet as well as light complexions. They have maidservants to wait on them and perform the principal part of the household work. Them [illegible] an abundance of leisure time ~~on their hands~~ and they are sometimes at a loss to know what to do with it. Unlike their fair and independent

~~and~~ or the reading to improve the mind.

Few have any children to attend to. And time does seem to hang rather heavy on their hands. Their two great amusements or methods of killing time are sipping beer and secretly smoking bang or indian hemp, as well as the men. They all take snuff. Although the men indulge pretty freely in smoking ~~bang~~ hemp they don't like their wives to follow their example, and many of them prohibit it. Nevertheless some do ~~all the women either~~ smoke it ~~bang~~, because it was caused a disease known by a minute eruption on the skin and ~~a speedy ... of habits informed us~~ quite incurable unless the habit be abandoned

It surprised them to learn that the English made cloth of the hemp instead of smoking it. We had ample opportunities of observing the effects of hemp smoking on our men. They said that it made them feel very strong ~~brave courageous~~ but It produced exactly the opposite effect

of bang smokers are singularly grotesque

They are provided with a calabash

of pure water, a split bamboo stick five

feet long and the great pipe which

is, a large bamboo chamber to contain

the water through which the smoke

is drawn Narghily fashion on its way to the mouth.

Each takes a few whiffs, ~~the last~~

and handing it to his neighbour, (the last

being an extra long one). The hideous

inspiration as he immediately takes a mouthful of water from the calabash, and a few seconds after he forces water and smoke from his mouth down the stem of the calabash to the ground

~~The~~ ~~Bang~~ Hemp smoke causes violent

and women especially at meal times for them they had the ~~Hawaiian~~ double alternative of fury, while men eat and of eating partaking with them. The men made an odd use of the spoon

We shocked the over refined sensibilities of the ladies by eating butter on our bread "Look at them! Look at them they are actually eating __raw__ butter right how nasty"! They could hardly have been more disgusted by seeing an Esquimaux ~~a Green-~~ ~~lander~~ eating raw ~~fat~~ tallow ~~...~~.

In their opinion butter is not fit to be eaten until it is cooked or melted [illegible] the body with it.

Polygamy, the sign of low civilization and source of many evils, is common, and singularly enough approved of even by the women who regard it as proper and desirable. On hearing that an English man could marry but one wife several ladies exclaimed Oh that's bad. They would not like to live in such a country, and could not

wives. Similar ideas prevail all down the Zambese. "No man is respected by the natives who has not several wives," a Portuguese gentleman once assured us. The reason for this is doubtless because he is wealthier than his neighbours, having the produce of each wife's garden.

Men and women begged hard

he liked the colour amazingly; When told he might have it for a mere two Karoos of Young Cocks, then he smiled and begged no more. A joke always stopped the begging.

The chiefs claim

The ~~[illegible]~~ humps & ribs of every ox slaughtered by his people and tribute of corn, honey, beer and wild fruits from the [illegible]

however is derived from ivory, while the

ivory of the Coast belongs to the chief

when the tusks of every elephant killed

are placed at his disposal. This

gives rise to differences [illegible] the

of the Portuguese and the natives around

where
there was here only one of the tusks belongs

being
to Government and the man is allowed

to retain the other, [illegible] would be

too
[illegible] claims all the ivory of his

nothing I have to the elephant, [illegible] At

Gentlemen [illegible] the [illegible] [illegible] of this
perturbation ~~struct~~ [illegible]

unit to [illegible] the elephants, but [illegible] some

taken up [illegible] to the change. He

was kept [illegible] prisoner [illegible] for three

months, and allowed to have the buffalo [illegible]

grass [illegible] [illegible] [illegible] machine

he pleased but the [illegible] the [illegible]

followed the [illegible] of the elephant to [illegible]

a keeper [illegible] [illegible] to [illegible] however, he

the opposite
in [illegible] direction, ~~Here~~ The change is

of the ivory with his people, as a father — may they as children require the guidance of their fathers against unscrupulous dealers, i.e. Foreigners — among his children. This binds to him all the upper classes who share the profits of the elephant hunt without undergoing much, if any, of the toil and danger of the chase. While the subject has not got the elephant['s] flesh which is all they ever had a taste for, none appears to have any wish to be Chief of the land. Our own men know

placed to, as far their labour had acquired

certain

these their ideas which they also learnt the

this old law

justice against, They thought it unjust

to be compelled to give up both tusks to

the chief; but as the Portuguese whom they

were not so oppressive as theirs, They always

allowed the hunter one of the tusks,

wrong

Sekeletu, thus his law, they wished

he would repeal it. This law doubtless

preserved the elephants though not

instituted with this object in view.

Pitsane shot a few on his return from

all together,

The three Makololo who returned recently from Benguela with the tails of the poor bewitched horses called on us after our arrival. "They had found out that all the Doctor told them was true, every word of it; They had

made clear the farmers presently getting
new clothes, they had before coming
They put on all they brought with them. They came
over
to see us, and were certainly better
dressed than we were ourselves. They
wore shirts with starched and ironed
white
bosoms, coats, and trousers, jackets
with
and patent leather shoes; and

him were by no means disposed to admit

that the travellers knew more than they

did. "They had seen the sea had they, and

what is that? Nothing but water. They

could see plenty of ~~that~~ water at home, more

than they wanted to see; and while

people came to their own town, they

at them. Justice appears to be
pretty fairly administered in the tribe.
A black headman took the beads and handkerchiefs
from one of his own men who had been with us.
The matter was brought before the Chief who
immediately ordered the goods to be restored
and decreed that (no headman should) take
the property of the men who had returned.
In theory all the goods brought back by the men
belong to the Chief, they lay them at his
feet and make a formal offering, then
he looks at the things & tells the men
and are almost invariably ~~requested~~ told to
to keep them.

might take a fancy to some of his best
goods, exhibiting one day a few of his least
valuable things. Mtesa having had
occasion to stop, having committed some
breach of native law in one of the villages
on the way, he paid a heavy fine rather
than have it brought to the Dorians.

Whilst Sekeletu [illegible] ox belonging to a
black man was killed by an ~~alligator~~ [crocodile]
Another man found the carcase floating
in the river and appropriated the meat –
When the owner heard of this he requested
the man to accompany him to the chief as
he meant to complain of him, ~~as the~~ [Rather]
than go before the chief, the man settled
the matter by giving him one of his own
oxen in place of the lost one.

alone, some of them must go back with you

Indians frequently leave their own

headman and flee to another village

and sometimes a whole village decamps

by night leaving the headman without

any people. The Administration never interferes

with the liberty of the subject to choose his

own headman as it is often the family of

headmen which causes their trouble

was ordered to [illegible] for Sekeletu
but he went off and I had hunger for two
days. Once for this he was doomed to die
He was carried in a canoe to the
middle of the river and choked as
towed with the stream, The spectators [illegible]

We met a venerable warrior Sile Milburn

portraits of the Mantatee host when ~~when~~
threatened to invade
the colony in 1824 he retains a vivid

recollection of their encounter with the

Griquas "As we looked at the masses

horses puffs of smoke came and our

men dropped down dead ~~all about~~ Never saw

prince of which people are [illegible]."

The ancient Costume of the Makololo con-sisted of the Litoni, the skin of the jerboa or other small animal worn under the loins, and a Karoso which was thrown over the shoulders in cold weather. The Karoso is now laid aside and all the young fashionable dandies wear a monkey jacket

of civilization seems to lead us successively on to another. The possessing of clothes creates a demand for soap; give a man a needle and he is soon back to you

The wife of Pulime was busy building

a large hut which we saw in the town.

She informed us that the men left

housebuilding to the women and being

a round tower of stakes, and 8 or 9 or

10 ft high is built & plastered, a floor

is next made of soft clay and ...

soil and come up through the floor

The bile causes fever in form of damp

fever in all, The roof is made [illegible]

and thatch on the ground and then

lifted up (many persons, women,) and placed on the tower

els, (plastered) and fences built up to meet

the roof which projects a little over it

leaving a space of three feet between

them & the house and the fence, the

The inner door of the hut we occupied was 19¼ inches high at the centre, the top being rounded off. And 22½ inches wide at the bottom. 12 inches from the bottom it measured 17½ inches in breadth and 3 inches from the top it was only 12½ inches wide, it was a difficult matter to get through it. The middle of this tower has no light nor ventilation except

is peculiar. A little girl is carried on
~~outspread arms~~
the shoulders of two with ~~her~~ ~~arms spread~~
her arms outstretched and while she walks about
in the ring all the rest clap their hands &
sing several very pretty airs. They stop
before each but be sing, some beat time
on their little kilts of cowskin and
others make a curious humming sound

have great faith in the power of medicine. They believe that there is a special medicine for every ill that flesh is heir to.

Mamere is anxious to have children; he has six wives ~~but~~ only one child, and he begs earnestly for child-medicine.

The mother of Sekeletu has come from the Barotse valley to see her son thinks she has lost flesh since the Doctor was here before and asks for the medicine of fatness. The Makololo women think

when we were coming He at once sent a messenger for them This man returned on the 7th day, having walked two hundred & forty geographical miles. One of the packages was too heavy for him and he left it behind. As the Dr wished to get

turn a house as here. Every thing in

his reign is just the same as when he left it

seven years before. The house made

him cordially welcome and lamented that they

had so little to offer ~~him~~ ~~in the way of~~

the ~~hunger~~, had he only come seven years

before when there was an abundance of milk

and cream. At midnight the town

In the year 1853 Dr L. started from Linyanti with the intention of opening up a path from the interior to the west coast, Being all uncertain whether he should live through the hazardous journey he left with the Makololo two volumes of his notes and a letter to be given

Ngami; the other his notes on natural history gathered from his own observations years, & from information gathered up from time to time from the Bushmen of the desert and from the careful observation of W. C. Oswell Esq. in whom he had many conversations for the sake of doing, which he

friend who had most faithfully & devotedly

carried all his property, told him that

~~[illegible] Two~~ Two only

~~Edwards and Chapman~~ from the Cape

came to the country in his absence from the Cape,

~~[illegible]~~ them – And they ~~had~~ given the

volumes, letters ~~to Edwards~~ to ______ X When he

reached England & thought of writing a

narration of his travels, he wrote to Mr

Moffat to make enquiry of ~~Edwards~~ as to

the manuscripts but the trader declined

wagon by a headman at Liriyankati. The
headman on being interrogated said he gave
them to ~~Edmund~~. But he says that he
never received them. "He lies" then exclaims
the headman's wife for I saw him take
them myself". Whether these conversations
are going on, oddly enough the Natural
history volume was actually in the Dr's

He was supposed to possess. No one can suspect Chapman for he was not implicated until long subsequent to this he himself published a volume of travels in which natural history is pretty fully discussed since, having notes of his own, he would, therefore, care no more for another man's notes than the [illegible]

bag from Mountkalsi's country, but there was no Greek volume inside when it left his hands. Singularly enough Mr Edwards happened to be in Mountkalsi's country at the very time this bag left. The other volume has never come to light

X Stokoltons head th

absolutely refused to leave his den and appear in public, till he was per-fectly cured and had regained what he considered his original good looks

As we expected the new Steamer from England would be at the Kongone in November it was impossible for us to remain at Sesheke more than a month

paddles for the road he brought. Two

young Makololo and Sesuntu to take down

and bring a supply of medicine for

were directed to feel the way but as we in-

his disease - and see if we could not

surmount the rapids of Kebrabasa

tended to purchase canoes at Senna,

the Chief sent his adigar with canoes

to paddle us down the river. He gave

us also a few oxen to eat on the path,

Our Cook petitioned to be allowed to return

gone back to the ~~[illegible]~~ out [illegible] [illegible]
~~the [illegible]~~ to [illegible] [illegible] as far as possible
Since it [illegible] had become thoroughly convinced
that the English system of paying a
man for his labour was the only correct
one, and all, except the single Matabele
headman thought it would be better for
them to be under a government where
they could sell their labour for what it
was worth.   Which is the history

and not only maintained decorum them

happened

-selves but insisted on the natives, who happen

Betika

to be present during the service, of a chief ~~att~~

came

~~a body of his men~~ ~~[illegible]~~ on one occasion

with a number of his men. They listened

in silence to the reading of the word of God

but as soon as we all knelt down to pray

-their mode of asking a favour by

commenced a vigorous clapping of ~~their~~

hands. The indignant Makololo [illegible]

them to groups of admiring friends.

Their ideas of right and wrong doubtless differ
in no respect
from our own except perhaps in their pro-
-fessed inability to see how it can be
improper or even indecent for a man
to have more than one wife when he

for them. They must wait a little longer
be hunted, but but a number of oxen
that the Et would, return with their

-pidity, he had his servant Jeller, but on account of his attendance on his boy who had been very much neglected.

X He had three small canoes to carry our baggage and ourselves to Mtolele, below which is a rapid dangerous to canoe navigation. The men went on foot. By day the canoe men are accustomed to keep close under the channel bank

stream as there these animals are close to bank on their way to their feeding places

Our progress was considerably impeded by the high winds which at this season of the year begin about eight in the morning and blow strongly up the river all day.

The canoes were poor leaky affairs and so low in some parts of the gunwale that the paddlers were afraid to follow the channel when it crossed the river

river when the waves run high. Still
though timid
they are by no means unskilful canoemen
It rather astonished ~~Hom~~ our party afterwards when
they saw the admirable way the Makololo
or young men managed their canoes on a
way to Tette and even amongst the breakers
They never dream that the like of that was
possible. On the night of the 17th
we slept on the left bank of the Mazaro
after ferrying all the men across
Also one man, Hampstead, [illegible] and [illegible]

it was left next morning. Our two young
Makololo companions, Moloko & Rama-
-kukane having never travelled before
naturally cling to some of the customs
they have been accustomed to at home;
when they lie down to sleep
their servants are called ~~at~~ ~~[illegible]~~ to
spread their blankets over ~~them~~ ~~when~~
roll together their feet
these august persons ~~lie down~~ to ~~sleep~~
This is the duty of the Makololo wife when
her husband is at home. Perhaps the

Slept one night at the village of [illegible]

When [illegible] along [illegible] [illegible] of

the news of this headman [illegible] came at once

came carefully and kindly spread his

blanket over him. A beautiful

silvery fish with a black spot, called

the Nguena is very abundant in the

river. Some large ones weigh 15 or 20 lbs.

The [illegible] are [illegible] and [illegible]

like wire cutters. He seems to be a poisonous fish as they are frequently found floating dead. Our canoe men picked up dead fish invariably they ate the dead in the [illegible] however few fish. A loud smell is no objection. The fish was boiled in water and the water drunk as soup. It is a common fact that ~~[illegible]~~ many ~~[illegible]~~ ~~[illegible]~~ Africans ~~[illegible]~~ ~~[illegible]~~ keep the fish until they getting them into their feet but the Makololo cannot do so, ~~with~~ The reason as explained to us, by the Makololo is, that these people have a medicine which renders the flesh bones, proper to pierce their feet, but they will not tell the Makololo what the medicine

by, on the left, Taking advantage of

the fog continued through till they ~~had~~

set fire to the reeds between the Chile

and Tumbes in such a manner as to

drive ~~and~~ the game out at one corner

where his men lay in wait with their

house; They [illegible] peculiar appearance in their looks, and [illegible] the [illegible] another fell out [illegible] but three left.

A Makololo gentleman who accompanies us to the falls is a great admirer of the ladies. Every pretty girl he sees fills his tender heart with rapture 'Oh what a beauty' Looked her hearts — never saw her like before. I wonder if she is married

And earnestly & long, does he gaze after the steamer going on till she has passed out of sight. He has four wives at home but he hopes to take [illegible] more before long. The Batoka Chief Moshobotwane again treated us with the usual hospitality of his generous race, giving us an ox, meal & milk. The tusk and the [illegible] of the Grand

assisted in placing a fence round the

so much power is allowed to underlings

Garden ~~that the~~ he appears ~~to~~ have cast off (as if he)

the authority of Sekeletu ~~and~~ does not

~~Others~~ ~~love~~ shew the usual courtesy to his messengers

Instead of giving them food as is cus-

-tomary he took the meal out of the

pot and handed it to his own people

Some of the natives here are at ~~Seshk~~ Seshekè

coming up to a piece of the [illegible] of

Baskets appear whitewashed here commonly

the lower half filled with bran.

Eggs are a perilous investment; the

native idea of a good egg and our own

appear as wide, as it is possible they could

on such a small subject. An egg is far

appetizing though is

with an embryo chick inside and even

when the interior is in a more objectionable

of Bakwini under

of Machumesi. It is built on a low

ridge of loose red soil which produces

great crops of Holcus sorghum and groundnuts

There are many magnificent fruit trees

near the village. Machumesi possesses

a herd of cattle and "is a large heart"; he

kept us company for a couple of days

to guide us on our way. At the Falls we

were told of another and deeper cleft a few

miles below. The Zambesi near this

upper end,
and a high ridge, running south a few miles
below the Chimney the river appeared to give
support to the story. We crossed the country
to learn a look at the river right again
suddenly disappearing in the earth
but when we looked
~~but instead of that we saw on looking~~
the bank in length the dam
down, 800 ft, ~~beneath~~ nothing but the
quiet river gliding round the foot of the
historic hill instead of underneath
it. Another great Fall however
exists two miles, below which ...

its Small and insignificant Rapids
We were ~~told~~ deceived and perhaps deserved to
be. One Mountain range is enough
for a Continent. The natives
of Africa have an amiable desire
to please one and often say what they
think will please, rather than what
is true. A native from the interior

Seen on their lips? Simsi! Yes, like
the same answer would have been
given had he asked for gold or gum
gil. English sportsmen, though ~~copal~~ (copal)
good
excellent shots at home generally miss
a good deal at first until their eyes
get accustomed to measuring distances
in an African atmosphere.
"Did I hit it?" enquired a gentleman
of his black attendant, after firing at an antelope. "Yes! You
hit it right here," pointing to the heart.

but no one had a similar experience ~~the~~ ~~gentlem~~

at b.

Upon asking, his friend who understood the

circumstances he reached

language pretty thoroughly, the following?

tell him truly. "Oh," said the native

I thought he would be angry if I told

him the truth; he never hits at all."

We had an opportunity of seeing a little

more of the Basotha during this trip.

They did not reach till evening before getting

Hungerford. The aged wife of the head-

-man of a hamlet (where we rested a few

ones to make us some porridge. There are but few good looking young women in all the Batoka villages round the Falls The Makololo marrying all the pretty girls ~~that the race of Batoka deteriorates in this region~~ ~~A quiet subdued air of sadness sits on each countenance as though they keenly feel their abject condition~~

~~The subjugation of these people by the Makololo can hardly be regarded otherwise than as a calamity. It has~~

~~done the congress no good. And the bills~~

~~much harm; Sublime having led~~

~~a Monastery life for Many years, knowing~~

~~about nothing in the place she thought whom~~

~~the inspired Oracle was perfectly divine -~~

~~Even the Feminine "I am fleeing -~~

~~from the Masticator" to blue the boot the~~

~~[illegible] the country, They totally~~

most native

~~[illegible] the people [illegible] their country,~~

~~[illegible] (freed from~~

~~[illegible] they came [illegible] but~~

~~they did not Mistake him. [illegible]~~

~~time he suspected that they meant to~~

~~attack him [illegible] large [illegible] of [illegible]~~

~~enemy he attacked them [illegible] with his~~

~~[illegible] a~~

~~peaceable people accustomed only to agri-~~

~~cultural pursuits. Plassy~~

~~however the real cause of the [illegible] the~~

~~[illegible] Nabob [illegible],~~

~~of [illegible] The Battle~~

~~[illegible] the [illegible]~~

~~[illegible]~~

~~[illegible] of Calcutta [illegible]~~

~~in the South. When Sebitoane was~~

~~driven out of the Batoka country by the~~

~~Matebele he could not take with~~

~~of the cattle with him. After the Makololo~~

~~were [illegible] however he sent for the~~

~~Batoka who had taken refuge in the~~

~~Machina hills to come and take them,~~

~~Many of the cattle with them, perished~~

The ~~[illegible] day that began Sebitoane~~

~~conquest the Batoka~~ confess that they ~~were intensely~~

~~inhospitable and used to kill all~~

~~strangers. And killed their heads~~

ples [illegible] these villages. If the, were

to do so a few years ago it is beyond

measure gratifying to witness the wonderful

change which has come over them.

They have passed, in the same generation

from the [illegible] extreme of barbarism, inhospitality

to the opposite extreme of kindly, sympathy,

And open handed generosity, otherwise

the heathen, of the [illegible] whole two

hundred Islanders are now converted professors

of [illegible] [illegible] 40

[illegible] transformed, But [illegible]

-ordinary

the, ugly –

~~[illegible] the [illegible] [illegible] [illegible] [illegible] of the [illegible]~~

~~[illegible] [illegible]~~

~~[illegible] [illegible] [illegible] [illegible]. It was not [illegible] [illegible]~~

~~[illegible] [illegible] [illegible] [illegible] of [illegible] the~~

~~[illegible] [illegible] of that it was [illegible] [illegible]~~

~~[illegible] [illegible] [illegible] [illegible]~~

~~[illegible] [illegible] many of them; [illegible]~~

~~the [illegible], of the [illegible] [illegible] the [illegible]~~

~~of the [illegible] [illegible] [illegible] [illegible]~~

~~[illegible] [illegible] old customs. The~~

~~[illegible] [illegible] the death penalty, [illegible]~~

~~[illegible] not put a stop to the habit~~

~~of [illegible] [illegible] [illegible] [illegible]~~

~~the [illegible] of [illegible] boys [illegible]~~

without them teeth the Ancient could not

be once learned how they lost them,

To drive a people through the [illegible]

of adversity; to rob them of cattle, country

and all their possessions is a surface way

of making them hospitable to strangers.

The [illegible] of the [illegible]

character [illegible]

ora They [illegible]

Danger, that [illegible]

Death, the [illegible]

it — The [illegible] portes at the of

~~their villages but they [illegible] not the skulls~~
~~of strangers but of [illegible] enemies who~~
~~have murdered their own [illegible]~~
~~their friends.~~ In one village ~~we~~ saw an
alligator's head on a pole. It had got
into the inclosure constructed to protect the
women when drawing water, and caught a
woman. The men rushed to the rescue
killed the monster and stuck his head on
a pole as they were wont to do with the heads ~~of all their~~.

Strangers ~~Cannibals.~~

As strong a clannish feeling
as among all the tribes
exists among the Batoka. Those belong

and are ~~[illegible]~~ ~~remarkably~~ kind to one another

The Batoka excel in following the spoor of a wounded animal. ¶/ Our path on the way back lay nearer the Zambesi than that by which we went up, 21 days over a rougher country with many hills and perennial streams. We encamped on the Kalomo on the 1st of Oct. and found the weather very much warmer

~~from~~ feet from the ground was 101° in the shade; the wet bulb being only 61° the a difference of 40° between the wet and dry bulbs. Yet notwithstanding this extreme dryness of the atmosphere not a drop of rain having fallen for months and no dew. Many of the shrubs and trees appear in fresh ~~green~~ leaves of various hues ~~just out~~ while others making a gorgeous clothing of lovely blossom.

I saw the sites of ruined Bab the village

is not yet ripe and we are unable to

say whether Europeans would be coloured
Any catallee part of uncultivated fruits is
as highly as the natives do. Africans
usually very small and as
who have never seen a hill except an ant-

-hill are struck with the size of very

heights
insignificant ~~ones~~ ~~and~~ and the most highly

extolled of their fruits may be no great

things after all. One of our men

opened an eel in the Kalomo which

round the neck. Two old and amazingly savage buffaloes were shot on the 3rd. One fell on receiving a piece of shell and two rifle balls, it lost a large amount of blood yet sprang up and charged a native with great ~~furiousness~~ agility. Fortunately he had just time to spring up a tree, when up the maddened beast came and struck the tree hard enough to have split both tree and head. It paused a few

him out of it. It took two great shells and five solid rifle balls to bring it down. There had been three of these old surly buffaloes wandering about in a sort of mutual fellowship; their horns were worn down nearly to stumps.

On the 6th we came upon the Yellow Sandstone, having entered the vast coal field which extends from

of 400 miles. Some writers tell us that the Coal measures of England will be worked out in two or three centuries after which there will be a decline and fall of the British empire. Here however is Coal enough to supply her furnaces for centuries yet to come and should Portugal live to see the 20th century She will surely then abandon the dog in the manger policy she clings to at this

resources of the continent, and give the people the blessings of the Christian religion and the Christian civilization.

Sinamane is the ablest and most capable of the Batoka chiefs we have met; he was independent till lately ~~too, the~~ when he sent in his adhesion & all that Sekeletu asks of him ~~being~~ is to furnish the Makololo with canoes when they wish to cross the Zambesi to attack — He will probably continue loyal. ~~the [illegible] We see many [illegible]~~ ~~Leshore's mission was to ratify this~~

Cooking young women now. Mariana
of his own Batoka countrymen calling
parties never tender here, having called
themselves Makololo
of Sinamane, big spear, Bejeso,
Batoka
A little chief named Mashikosa was one of a
party that came to steal some of the
young women but Sinamane and then
attacked him [illegible] then so
furiously that the survivors [illegible]
on the [illegible] Mashikosa had to run for
his life & in fact that there among his shield

Sinamane's people cultivate large quantities ~~on the damp banks of the river~~ of tobacco, which they manufacture into balls for the Makololo market; twenty balls weighing about 3/4 lb each are sold for a hoe. The tobacco is planted on low moist spots on the banks of the Zambesi, it is in flower at present, Sinamane's ~~his~~ people appear to have abundance of food and are all ni-

[illegible] about 250 yds wide and flows
between high banks
serenely to the S.E. Every damp
spot is covered with maize, pumpkins,
water melons, tobacco and hemp, and
there is a pretty numerous Barotse population
on both sides of the river. They saluted
us from the banks as we passed by
clapping their hands, A headman

the received a handsome present of corn and fattest

the great one have ever seen, it resembled

Mutton, this people were as liberal as

their chief. They brought two large baskets of

corn and a lot of tobacco as a kind of

general contribution to the travellers.

before the stipulated time, he went back with the story, that the white men had stolen the canoes. Shortly after sunrise next morning Sinamam came into the village with 50 of his long spears, evidently determined to retaliate. Before

he had been deceived by his followers, a strange
cause the foolish fellow
remark it of his, and the ~~foolish~~ to learn
fighting and
meddling with encounters, in could fall
~~and~~ fighting ~~battles~~ As Simon and
had been very kind to us and made him
an additional present of a few things of the
white goods, November something the past
good friends. When bargaining for
for canoes
~~canoes~~ with November, we were grateful
to observe that he wished to deal with us
and
not any fancy ~~but~~ even honourable gentlemen

only two spare canoes; One was good

the one he would sell to us; the other he would

not sell to us because it had a bad

trick of capsizing and spilling whatever

was inside into the river; he would lend

us his two large ones until we could buy

others below. The best canoes are

made from the Acacia tree; these are

[illegible] in fruit. Some of the natives boil

the pods in water and mix them with

were having a gay time, singing, dancing, and drinking ~~their~~ celebrating beer. At once a large pitful was brought in. The chief spoke but little; his orator did the talking and smiling for him and seemed anxious to show how cleverly he could do both.

This is in advance of the Portuguese, for though many women are annually carried off by alligators at Sena and Tette so little are the lives of these poor drawers of water valued by the Portuguese they never think of erecting even a single fence for their protection, Dr L tried to induce the Padre of Tette to move in

padre merely smiled, shrugged his shoulders, and did nothing. Beautiful Cranes, are are seen daily; they are beginning to pair. Large flocks of black geese are common also pairs of the Egyptian geese are ~~[illegible]~~ ~~[illegible]~~ ~~[illegible]~~, as well as a few Knob nosed geese. In some places the steep banks are dotted with the holes of Bee-eaters, which

One gives a goat and the other fowls or

maize, ~~[illegible]~~

they now these Batoka
believe that ~~they~~ their hearts, though

at first they were to the expense of them
for and subjected Batoka
outstanding parties of Makololo had

formed, made troops in several tribes
as those who inflict an injury usually do
of them ... and Moloka ~~[illegible]~~
blamed them for
~~[illegible]~~ hating the Makololo and killing

every one they met. ~~He came up to a~~

~~[illegible]~~ a few mornings since he appeared

in great grief and feared his servant

Rhengea had disappeared the day before

he was sure that the Batoka had caught &

killed him. In a few minutes,

his Rhengea ~~came up~~ arrived with the ten men

who had ~~they~~ found him wandering, after much

gave him supper and lodging and brought

him on to us, carrying his load for him.

On the morning of the 12 we passed

through a wild hilly & ~~wooded~~ ~~[illegible]~~ [illegible]

~~with numerous~~ hills on both sides, ~~the~~ but

few inhabitants. We took breakfast

at Mpende's, whose large island ~~supports~~

with the villages and ~~[illegible]~~ lies opposite the

mouth of the ~~Zu~~ Zungwe when we

left the Zambesi on our way up.

Mpende was sorry that he had no

canoes of his own to sell to us but he

would lend us two; he gave us cooked

pumpkins and watermelons and

~~came with~~ accompanied us till we had an opportunity

We paid what was, considered a large price for it, viz. seven strings of blue cut glass neck ~~glass~~ beads two large blue ones, like marbles, and two yards of grey calico ~~blue cloth~~. The trading party of Sequarahs, which we met one day had purchased ten large new canoes for six strings of cheap coarse white beads apiece or the equivalent four yards of calico ~~fine cloth~~, and had bought for the merest trifle ivory enough to load them all. These fellows had been living in

part of Africa and will soon change
the character of the inhabitants.
And lions are remarkably numerous
in some places, and even where but few
were are to be seen. These patient
beasts are said to have a great deal of
attraction at this season of the year

the river small rapids occasionally
which are probably not in existence during
the rest of the year. We went down
three small rapids on the 17th and
came on the morning of the 19th to the

Peter & Alex in the other two Canoe-
-men were afraid to see him among
them, because they suppose there
is commonly an alternative one in a
man which takes a malignant pleasure
in upsetting canoes. We fired a

and said that there was a man on his
side who knew how to pray to the
Kamba gods and advised us to hire him
to pray for our safety while we were
going down the rapids or we should
certainly all be drowned. Soon

could not (unsure), if they would come
over to his side, then he might be able
to see them. We crossed but he
went off to the village. We then
turned and walked over the hills
to have a look at Kuruba before
venturing our canoes in it. The
current was ~~strong~~ and there was ~~the water~~

village while we were gone and were treated to beer and tobacco. The man who knows how to pray, to the devils who rule the rapids followed us with several of his friends and were rather surprised to see us pass down in safety without the aid of his intercession to gods which our men now concluded were not worth the dead animal. As there was considerable current there and the rocky banks unfit for our camp we took the hippo in tow telling them to follow us and we would give them most of the meat;

The ~~alligators~~ crockodiles tugged so hard at the hippo to avoid upsetting a canoe we therefore were soon obliged to cast it adrift to float down in the the current

The country of Kariba Kariba is nearly as Kebrabasa

and returned to the village. We slept two nights at the place where the hippo was cut up. The ~~alligators~~ crockodiles had a busy time of it during the night tearing away at what was left in the river and thrashing the water furiously with their powerful tails.

The animal was a female and fat; it was ten feet in length and four feet one inch in height. Though the

a narrow channel for a number of miles

there are no more rapids; the river is

smooth and apparently very deep.

Only a single human being was seen, the

country being too rough for culture, the

Gum trees near the outlet of Kanbanana
(inserted above: "stamp in")

[illegible]

Good, Chikumbura. An hospitable old headman under the Chief Shomokela the paramount chief of a large district whom we did not see brought us a great basket of meal and four fowls "to make it taste good"; and brought a cake of fine meal in morning; his people seem to be well off. A few days before they caught three buffaloes in pitfalls in one night and left one being unable to eat them

trouble them by eating up their cotton plants

~~"They told Joseph that Mr. Oliphant's~~

~~"he would do so gladly but he has no~~

~~gun" Come with us to settle and we~~

~~will give you one "I am Shomatolas~~

~~Negro and cannot go with the Colloques~~

~~lend him first"!~~ Game quite kind

is in most extraordinary abundance

Time the, take in the Kafue, especially

and so it is

in the Mushikala's side when they are

night back running along through the

country swarming with wild animals,

vast herds of Pallahs, many waterbuck

Koodoos, buffaloes, wild pigs ~~and~~ elands

~~Impys~~ Zebra and Monkeys! Francolin

And Guinea fowl And myriads of pigs

with the fresh spoor of Elephants & Rhino

which had been All the [illegible] day & night,

security, always unreachable, the pre-
-caution of the few, first above the
deep channel into which they come
plunge unlearned Thence

hippopotamus in a herd. Our men had never seen the like before. It was of a pinkish white exactly like that of the albino or white negro. He seemed to be the father of a number of the others, for they were marked with large patches of

~~has a deficiency of~~ the colour,

~~matter in the vegetable products of the Cape~~

beautiful tree covered

also, the banks at the islands of

Juba Mokoro

Kalabi, opposite where ~~[illegible]~~ ~~Magos~~

believes the reason, lion are in [illegible]

There are many tame pigeons in the

A solitary hippopotamus has

village, ~~Something has been seen~~

selected the little bay on which we land

& where the women draw water for his dwelling

~~[illegible] all the way~~, & Pretty little

place.

and red

Lizards with light blue tails running

-form good service to man by eating great

numbers of the destructive white ants

~~an. the [illegible], with red back, is also com[illegible]~~

At noon of the 24th we found Sequasha

in a village with the main body of his

said ~~that he~~ 210 elephants had been
people; he ~~[illegible]~~ killed during this trip

The numbers of animals soon renders
~~210 elephants~~, many of his men ~~being~~
[illegible] possible

a
[illegible] hunters. After reaching the

he ~~he [illegible]~~ reports ~~that~~.
Kafue he went south and entered the

~~who appeared somewhat giddy, but~~
~~rejected his cloth instead and wished~~
~~to exchange it for young women, which~~
~~are the only goods they purchase. Some~~
~~misunderstanding took place between~~
~~them and he fired 10 guns at them~~
~~and carried away.~~ Seguar has is the
quarter Portuguese trader we are
acquainted with and brought ~~after~~ ~~that~~ he is
able to speak a dozen different dialects ~~languages~~ ..

meager account of the country & the people, he may have been, and his statements are not reliable. Among his stock of goods ~~[illegible]~~ were cheap American clocks, ~~[illegible]~~ a useless investment for ~~the~~ a people ~~[illegible]~~ of Africa where no one ~~[illegible] read the figures on the face, or~~ cares ~~they about~~ for the artificial measurement of time. ~~[illegible]~~

His clocks got him into trouble

meaning with the many Agencies at work to
bring all manner of evil upon honest people
Disquieting these, accused has been guilty

of a Milando and had to pay a heavy

fine of cattle & beads for his habits

of ticking clocks. He alluded to one

having heard that he had killed a Mpanya

and denied having actually done ~~this~~ ~~[illegible]~~
but in his absence
~~[illegible]~~ his name ..

got mixed up in the affair ~~his~~, in Con-
-sequence of the wrongdoing of his slaves,
~~who had told~~ Telling Nama Kuzoro while
drinking beer ~~with him~~ one night that
they would go and kill the chief for him.
His partner had not thought of this
when our friend Kum[?] on coming up for -
he tried to excuse the murder by saying
that now they had put the right man
in. ~~Sequently, he accused [illegible]~~

Waters we held ~~our way, that intends to~~

~~Carry a number of young women not~~

~~begin to trouble them for trying~~

The Zambesi is full of islands

here. On these are many buffaloes &

pursued, attracted hither by the fresh

young grass. We shot one on the former

of the 27th. ~~There was~~ Instead thunder was heard during

the night and the meat spoiled in as usually happens in this condition of the air.

In fact, the [illegible] not fit to eat [illegible]

next morning: hunger however with no choice but, want, makes

of salutations, ~~a little prostration~~

~~They~~ to clasp~~ed~~ the ~~thigh~~ hip with one

hand while approaching and on ~~after~~

~~after~~ sitting down before us. ~~There~~

~~was~~ the same clasping took place when they handed

the present to our men ~~and~~ when they

received a present ~~in return~~ and

also on their departure. ~~They clasp~~

~~the thigh, the hand, etc. when...~~

~~that it was desperately [illegible] the little~~

~~[illegible] [illegible] that they must~~

~~[illegible] for his family and~~

~~if this had been the case they would~~

~~have fled into the woods where~~

~~[illegible] till they had passed.~~

After 3 hours sail on the morning of the

29th the river ~~[illegible]~~ narrowed again

into one channel and with the rapid

appearance. In going down this rapid

the men sent by Sekeletu ~~of one of the canoes~~ behaved u-

in a noble way the canoe

~~[illegible]~~. As it entered the

rapid a huge wave jobbling of mid current ~~rolled over and fille~~ filled ~~the canoe~~ it

it. With great presence of mind and without a moment's hesitation one of the frightened ill-fated individually jumped overboard, and adding the third many a Batiste told the same to the white man must be saved, "I can't swim" said the Batiste "jump out an hold on to the canoe." Swimming alongside they contrived to guide the swamping canoe down the swift current to the foot of the rapid where the other canoes waited to assist ~~assisting getting~~ it ashore, goes carries about a hundred yards.

As the sun was ~~dropping~~ brings the last canoe down

Clears the shore the stern swinging into the 6 knot current. All then was swept out into the middle of the river. Having held on when he ought to have let go, he next signalised himself by letting go when he ought to have held on; and was swallowed up in a few seconds by a roaring whirlpool; his comrades pushed out in a canoe below and caught him as he rose to the surface the third time

has the same shining black glaze on the surface. Many small baobabs adorn the hill sides, their fresh young leaves just out. There is no blade of ~~even dry grass on some of the hills~~ it being the end of the dry season ~~after a~~ succeeding a severe drought. And yet they are dotted over with beautiful green trees. A few antelopes were seen on the upper sides of a hill where a few people were [illegible] the ground for a crop of [illegible]. The Mbaruma narrows may be 20 miles in length. ~~We~~ We ~~were at the~~ arrived at Zumbo at the mouth of the Loangwa on the 1st of Novr. Our men waded the river with ease, the water

the ball lodging in the spleen, ~~[illegible]~~ and found to have ~~[illegible]~~ been shot in the spleen some ~~[illegible]~~ time previously, ~~he found~~ an in bullet was embedded in it, ~~the~~ and the wound ~~very~~ entirely healed.

A great deal of the plant is floating in the river at present. ~~There are~~ many people inhabit the right bank now, ~~still~~ yet the same

Mambo Kazai came with men, muskets & large powder horns to levy black mail and obtain payment for the wood we used in cooking breakfast. But we are English we said Oh are you, he thought we were Bazungus (Portuguese) they were the people he took payment from. And apologized for his mistake

Bazungu is applied to all ~~Though Bazungus means~~ white men as ~~general as~~ the Portuguese are the only white men these people have ever seen–

~~As we had~~ no desire to pass for Portuguese

quite the contrary, we ~~had to~~ usually made a ~~flat land that~~ broad enough line of demarcation by saying we ~~were~~ were English, ~~that~~ and the English did not buy ~~people~~ nor sell nor hold black people as slaves, and worked to put a stop to the slave trade altogether.

We called on our friend Mpende in passing; he provided a hut for us, having new mats spread on the floor, but we told him we were hurrying on as the rains were near. "Are they near" eagerly inquired an old councillor "Another

time for the rains to commence and ^we saw ~~that the~~

We knew nothing

~~than~~ the usual indications ~~[illegible]~~

more than themselves - Some

~~higher and a different kind of [illegible]~~

take advantage of their credulity to

~~[illegible]~~

gain temporary applause but the

natives are usually shrewd

~~[illegible]~~

enough to detect some discrepancy

and no one is duped but the

~~The rains failed for the past years~~

white man himself -

[illegible] has been blamed for driving the clouds

during the past drought

away and had to pay a heavy fine to the

Pindora as an atonement for his offence

~~[illegible] a pretty [illegible] that~~

~~a jewel of [illegible]~~

thunderstorm, cold, rain as day, though,
and the Jumna had risen several inches,
and became light, chocolate coloured.

Greater ease: it was a prize fat meat

rejoiced in the hope of

all ~~...~~ of the fat for

with our hard dry cakes of native meal

butter. Our cook has cut a

cut a choice piece for dinner, but after

the carcase

with the utmost intelligence that it was

they had been hoodwinked

gone. ~~...~~ the men were very much

astonishing themselves ~~for~~ a number of

boring an seemed to ~~assistance~~

in rolling it ashore

~~...~~

& asserting ~~that~~
it was all shallow water. They rolled on
towards the land
~~water all~~ creeping over ~~the~~ finder, the
rope we had made fast to it ~~in the~~
as they said, an incumbrance, it was
~~[illegible]~~
unloosed
~~[illegible]~~
were
~~water~~. ~~They were~~ all shouting, and talking,
as loud as they could bawl when suddenly,
as the Banyai intended,
it plumped into a deep hole. ~~and~~
when the Makololo
~~were~~ finding, all jumped in after it.

a bean fowl for dinner and glad enough to travel to get that. The hippo, however, floated during the night and was found about a mile below. The Bawenjai assembled on the bank and disputed our right to the ~~beast~~, "it might have been shot by somebody else". Our men took a little and left it rather than come into collision with the natives

the Kakobi natives, an enormous ~~alligator~~ crocodile had been eying him for the moment and ~~appears to have touched his leg~~ as he dropped beside the creek where he was feeding, it seized and dragged him into the water which was not very deep. The mortally wounded animal made a desperate plunge and hauling the ~~alligator~~ crocodile several yards tore himself out of its horrid jaws. To escape the hunter the antelope jumped into the river and was swimming across when another ~~alligator~~ crocodile gave chase to it

him as here. Below Ka Kalilo
and at the base of Mannyere-re-e Mountain
Outcrops of several Coal Seams (not seen on our ascent) crop out on the right

bank of the Zambesi. Chitora of

Chicova treated us with his former kindness

Our men were all much pleased with his kindness

When they come this way on a marauding

expedition to eat the sheep of the Banyai
for insulting them in the affair of the
hippopotamus
they will send word to Chitora not to

rapids at the East end of Chicoutimi
He broke up the canoes And went down a

The river narrowed into a groove 60 or
number of miles, until the navigation
~~30~~ 80 yards wide

became difficult and dangerous,
a fall of 15 feet had developed many
cataracts in our absence
Two of the canoes passed safely down a

dividing ugly
narrow channel which had a whirlpool
at the rocky partition between its two
~~[illegible]~~
branches — the hole in the whirlpool
opening & then shutting
The Dr's canoe commenced and seemed

open
to be drifting broadside into the whirlpool
the utmost exertions
in spite of ~~all~~ the men ~~[illegible]~~ with
their paddles
The men all looking at it expecting
to see ... saying "look where those people
going" "look, look"
had to rush to the rescue when a ...

173 a projection of the perpendicular
was dashed on the rocks by one of the

sudden & mysterious boiling up of the
occurs at irregular intervals,
water which ~~is of frequent occurrence~~ Dr K
resisting the sucking down action
of the water which must be 15 fathoms
~~[illegible]~~
deep got on the ledge while the
steersman ~~then~~ holding on to the same rock
saved the canoe while nearly
~~[illegible]~~. The
all its contents were swept
away down the stream
~~[illegible]~~, ~~[illegible]~~ few of the
were left in it
things but all that was valuable
including a chronometer, ~~[illegible]~~
~~[illegible]~~, a Barometer and
to our great sorrow Dr Kirk's notes
of the journey and Botanical drawings
of the leaf the interior or fruit trees [illegible]
sorry had not
foot ~~[illegible]~~ [illegible] we ~~should have~~ [illegible]

longer, but the fatigue of a day's march

over the hot rocks & having some changes

their horses before night. And they regretted

having left the canoes, thought they should

have dragged them past the dangerous

place, and then launched them again,

We met two large trading parties of
Tete natives on their way to Zumbo;
They had a number of Manganja women
with ropes round their necks and made
fast to one long rope, to be sold ~~[illegible]~~
for ivory. The headman of a few
hamlets below Kebrabasa were

in a loud voice called across the valley, on the women of the other hamlet, to cook supper for us. About 8 in the evening he returned followed by a procession of women bearing the food. There were 8 dishes of rice a porridge. 6 of different [illegible], of a curry, good [illegible] vegetables, with dishes of beans, and fowls, all in a [illegible] [illegible] and [illegible] of cheese. The wooden dishes were many in which the man

having been gone a little over six months,

The two English sailors left in charge of the ship were well and had enjoyed excellent health all the time we were away

Their farming had been a failure,

They left a few sheep to be slaughtered when they wanted meat and to complete and wash the vegetable garden,

The sheep broke into the cotton patch

where it was in flower an' eat all

except the stems, and then the ~~alligators~~ crocodiles

carried off the sheep and the water

stole the fowls. [illegible]

Colony, which has rusted off. "I think

I knows how I can one whose father

was a blacksmith." "It's very easy, you

have only to put the barrels in the fire

~~The Portuguese asked if he would do it~~

~~for him and~~ naturally, rather, to oblige

~~to undertook~~ the job. A great fire

of wood was made on shore and the

unlucky barrel, put over it ~~on the hearth to~~

to secure

~~it [illegible]~~ the handsome rifle

column. To Jack's utter amazement

~~out of the fire,~~ He went back to his Comrade

in trouble "This is the baddest scrape

ever I got into What shall we do"?

They stuck the pieces together with the

rosin And sent it home to the owner,

Says, it was they could do for it And they

would not charge him anything for fixing it.

refused to leave the ship till he got me

a chameleon, as, brought out of the

cabin. It was the moment the natives saw

this creature of which they have a mortal

dread they spread over board at once

The poor chameleon settled long disputes

in a twinkling.   A terrible scene

was then up one night. As they

pushed off in the boat to the rescue

crocodile   had caught a woman and

A terrible alligator ^ was dragging ~~a woman~~

re-

across a shallow sandbank just

off her leg at the knee, they took her

on board, bandaged the limb ~~[illegible]~~ as well

as they could and not thinking of any

better way of showing their sympathy for

the fair suffering woman gave her a glass of rum,

and carried her to her hut,

Next morning they found that the people

about her had torn off the bandages and

left her to die "Sheliu" is another one

Sending out Convicts as colonists, says

These men can never do anything for the country they know how to keep their arms clean but nothing else. Of what possible use was it to send agricultural implements for men like these"

The [illegible]

[illegible] at Tette

[illegible]

new leaks broke out every day; the engine
pumps gave way, the bridge broke down;
all three compartments filled at night
And in a few days we were assured that
of hearing "She can't be worse than she is
now." But on the morning of the 21st
the unfortunate Arithmetic grounded
& filled on a sand bank, she could
not be emptied nor got off; The river rose during
the night and all that was visible

We spent Christmas encamped on the island of Chumba. Canoes were sent for from Senna, ~~which place~~ and we reached it on the 27 ~~[illegible]~~ to be again hospitably entertained by our friend Senhor Ferrão. A large party of slaves, belonging to the Commandant had just returned from a trading Expedition to Moselekatse's ~~[illegible]~~ country after having been away the greater part of a year. They ~~took~~ had taken inland a thousand muskets, being, they said,

~~as~~ them ~~the~~ the only article, all calculated [illegible]

should a Kaffir war be got up there

these arms will of course be credited to the Missionaries.

Crowds to purchase ~~for these goods,~~

they had wrought each

~~a~~ ivory, ostrich feathers, a

thousand ~~[illegible]~~ & sheep and goats, and

head of Moselekatze

~~forty~~ fine cattle, ~~the chief~~ [illegible]

~~[illegible]~~ in addition the commandant

sent a splendid white bull to ~~[illegible]~~

as a token ~~that~~ the traders & he

~~[illegible]~~

~~And then~~, two parties parted. The article

feathers, ~~[illegible]~~ being all in sacks, – a few

broken on the camp [illegible]

187

to the Country; all the cattle died

the white ones perished within two days

from the effects of the bite [illegible] the herd

of Senna had been eaten

of the sheep & goats; ~~the white [illegible]~~

either because they became lame

~~two or~~ because the drivers were

hungry [illegible] the commandant

[illegible] habits [illegible] of [illegible]

was unable

[illegible] to calculate

his losses - but intended to

imprison the slaves who

~~[illegible]~~

as usual thought more

of their own comfort

~~the expedition had been [illegible]~~

than of their masters gain

Slip 187 We were at the

Kingani on the 4th of Jan. 1861; a

Flag Staff and a Custom house had

been erected during our absence,

-messing of the Linen Corporal who came to

see us as soon as he got ~~himself~~ into his

Trousers and Shirt, we took up our quarters

in the Cooking house which, like the

the other buildings is ~~barracks is~~ a small Square floorless hut of

Mangrove Stakes overlaid with ~~thatch~~ reeds

The soldiers complained of hunger; they had

nothing to eat but a little millet and

were making palm wine to deaden the

was written, our arrival at [illegible], seemed

were a year and a half old, ~~having been~~

~~practiced during the Administration being~~

~~Lord Derby~~ ~~There was~~ a good deal

It ~~is~~ was amusing to

~~of~~ ~~find~~ ~~at~~ reading article, written when

a prophetic fit had come up over ~~the~~

~~learned~~ an editor "Come what will

wrote an emphatic critic

~~and a Statist, quoted~~, "One thing

is absolutely certain Lord Salmon[illegible]

informed us that his Lordship was once

more at the head of H.M.'s Government,

~~Yet~~ weekly, Journal of rare valuability was

~~The succeeding number of~~ a weekly journal

of rare ability and ~~caustic~~ unreasonable bitterness

~~came for months until we found that~~

~~nothing unwholesome needed to be in the~~

~~Island into Africa; that ...~~

could not be read if we had

~~of that three already~~ some of us dared

a touch of jealousy

~~to read it on~~ ~~heaps of times~~; it caused much

191 one of

our party, who had never vomited in all

rashly Leader

his life tried to hear a ~~[illegible]~~ ~~aspen~~

~~as fever~~

was hovering over him ~~one afternoon~~. In

a few minutes his head was suddenly

thrust out of the cabin window ~~and the~~

vomiting ~~somewhat~~

~~waters of the [illegible] [illegible]~~

it was more than could be

~~[illegible]~~ ~~It is [illegible] [illegible]~~

borne to hear that

no English statesman is to be trusted

Earl Derby is bad, Lord Palmerston

is no better and John Bright ~~had the~~

deserved only

~~all the~~ thunderbolts ~~[illegible]~~

~~[illegible]~~. ~~It is not pleasant when~~

192

a whole absence having us suppose

somewhat the effect of time in history had led us to conclude

that all the great men of our country are better than the best of most other nations

---

Receiving afterwards other copies of this periodical we were gratified with the marked improvement of the caricatures ... our distinguished statesmen, ... no longer ... African fever ... indigestion.

~~He liked~~ Punch was a general favourite ... always genial and ...

welcomed at all times, ~~a delightful~~

His Essence of Parliament containing the best epitome of news ways

~~Companion [illegible]~~

read before all Newspapers & Great Tillers being a better preventative

the fevers ~~[illegible]~~

^ man quinine he did us good

by day

~~[illegible]~~ pleasant dreams

by night

~~which [illegible] the restless brain a~~

~~pleasing [illegible] wholesome form~~,

~~We read the Times advertisements when all other literature failed us And then [illegible] kept us [illegible] one dismal day. It is wonderful how much [illegible] one may derive from that [illegible]. There is a great~~

ounces of sugar, Coffee and tea were

expended ~~and heated~~ but scarcely, missed as our

vendors discovered a pretty good substitute

in roasted sorghum. Fresh meat was

obtained in abundance from our antelope

preserves on the large island below the

and some were from hundreds of yards inland. We had myriads of mosquitoes and some touches of fever ~~It is strange that~~ the men we brought from the ~~malarious~~ regions of the interior dropping almost as soon from it here ~~at the bar~~, as we did ourselves.

On the 31st our new ship the Pioneer anchored outside the bar, but the weather was stormy, and she did not come in

and five coloured men from the Cape,

It was rather a puzzle to know what to do with so many men, The estimable Bishop anxious to commence his philanthropic work without delay wished the Pioneer to carry the Mission up the Shire as far as Chibisa's and there leave them two months, he would have until the rainy season was half over. Then the Mission would be left in an unhealthy region, at the beginning of the sickliest season of the year, with no medical attendant, no knowledge of the language

flows out of Nyassa was a suitable place for the Mission. On the 25 the Pioneer anchored in the mouth of the Rovuma, which unlike most African rivers has no bar. We worked and then waited for the rising tide

our detention, The scenery on the

Rovuma near the sea is superior to that on the Zambesi

Eight miles from the ~~In an hour from the~~

mouth the Mangroves are left & a beautiful range

of well wooded hills, on each bank

of the river. On these ridges the

blackwood tree resembling ebony, grows abundantly

and attains a large size. ~~These~~

~~were~~ few people were seen and they did not

appear to be very well off.

much less, on account of the crossing,
there was barely water enough for the
ships drawing 5 feet to pass. When 30 miles up the
river the water fell suddenly four in
24 hours. As the march proceeds, the

I think it of and so concluded to return

to the Shire, see the Mission party

settled safely, and afterwards a place for the Scotch

and the ~~Lady~~ Nyassa upon the lake.

Fever broke out on board the Pioneer

in the mouth of the river, and ~~[illegible]~~

to [illegible] her until we completely ~~[illegible]~~
isolated the engine room from the rest
of the ship – the coal dust putrefying kept up
~~[illegible]~~
the fever for a twelve month afterwards.

Touching at Mohilla
One of the Comoro islands, ~~[illegible]~~

on our return we found

a mixed race of Arabs, Africans and

their conqueror, the natives of Madagascar

Being Mahometans ~~All profess the [illegible] religion~~; they have

mosques and also schools in which girls

as well as boys are taught to read the Koran. The

teachers are ~~that~~ paid ~~by the town but~~ by

the job; ~~the~~ usually two dollars for each

scholar taught to read. The clever ones learn

in a few months but the children take a

couple of years. The Mission, con-

-structed under the skilful supervision

of the late Admiral Washington, a

every respect except the ~~draught~~ of

water; She draws too much for the

navigation of the upper part of the Shire

during the dry three feet only she draw

wear fine   This unfortunate

mistake has caused us a great deal of
delay, and vexation, and brought the Captain
home and [illegible] in work, [illegible]

pleasantly, spent in exploring, in the region and otherwise usefully, all the objects of the expedition. ~~We were 40 days in getting up, 40 miles~~ ~~at last~~; On one we were a fortnight on a bank of gravel & shingle, stranded having, as it were, a river no less water than the ship drew; this was caused by the anchor coming home and the current setting the ship ~~drove~~ broadside on the bank which had formed behind

3 feet she could have run up and

down the river at any time of the year,

with perhaps one exception

but as it was, having once passed over a

few shallows near it, it was impossible

to take her down again until the river rose

in December. ~~The ship could~~ she could also go up

more or less the ~~thought it could~~ but not

under her

current barked away, from ~~the~~

bows we were daily visited by

crowds of natives who brought abundance

of provisions far beyond our ability to

purchase. In hauling the Prince

over the Shalem places the Bishop with

his men, ever ready and anxious to lend a

hand, worked as hard as any one on board.

Never before had we met with gentlemen

belonging to what is called the High Church

Party, but rumour has oft exaggerated!

in disguise or even living, the very leopards,
those serpents of the religious Mainland

Long before our friends left the ship
this had been the experience of the traveller
who saw through the early morning mist
which hung upon the mountain side
a frightful monster approaching him;
thoughts of the need of a pistol flashed
across his mind; but as the object
drew nearer and the mist began to clear
away he saw that it was only a number

but a Indian Agent when they find in the

plausible Inlight the man was his

own brother. We had friendly

interchange of views of an evening to

relieve the irksome monotony of the

forced detention in shore and banks.

ones we soon learned that with the single

exception of placing an exaggerated [illegible]

certain ordinary and harmless forms,
a higher value to
than Scotchmen in general are disposed

to do, Our friends differ in no respect

from the sterling characteristics of other nations!

and the [illegible], we invited them to return, he sent back the presents.

On reaching Chibisa, we heard that there was war in the Manganja country and the slave trade was going on briskly. A deputation from a chief near Zomba had just passed on its way to Chibisa who was, in a distant village, to implore him to come, or send medicine to drive off

partly of a [illegible], [illegible] [illegible] [illegible] [illegible]

[illegible] [illegible] [illegible] [illegible], [illegible] [illegible] few days before

we got the [illegible] [illegible]. [illegible] [illegible] head-

-men was [illegible] and [illegible], [illegible] permission [illegible] to carry [illegible] [illegible] [illegible]

to [illegible] as [illegible] [illegible] [illegible], as [illegible] willing to

go, [illegible] having [illegible] [illegible] a [illegible] [illegible]

number [illegible] started for the [illegible] on

the 10th of July, to shew the [illegible] the country which was

-sidered desirable for a station , Our first day,

obliged to go on till 4 p.m. when we
entered the small village of Chipinda
There was hunger in the village they said,
they had no food to sell and no kind place
to sleep in but if we went on, a
little further then we would come to a village
where they had plenty to sell; but we had
travelled far enough to and concluded to
remain where we were, before sunset

Mid forenoon we halted at the village
[illegible]
of Mbama to obtain some carriers as

Chobisa's men did not choose to go further.
After resting a little
Mbama told us that a slave party

would presently
[illegible] ~~was to~~ pass through his

interfere"?
village ~~that day~~. "Shall we ~~tolerate~~
we enquired of each other
~~[illegible]~~
We remembered ~~that~~ all our
valuable private baggage was in sight

of the Government property, and might be
in retaliation
destroyed as we passed the slaves, ~~[illegible]~~
but this system would so inevitably
thwart all the ~~[illegible]~~ efforts for which
~~[illegible]~~
we had the sanction of the Portuguese

213 Government ~~that~~ we resolved to run all risks and ~~[illegible]~~ put a stop if possible to the slave trade ~~which~~ had now followed ~~[illegible]~~ ~~[illegible]~~ on the footsteps of ~~[illegible]~~ our own discoveries.

~~In~~ A few minutes after Mbame had spoken to us the slave party, a long line of manacled men women & children came wending their way round the hill and into the valley. The black drivers armed with muskets and bedecked with various articles of ~~[illegible]~~ finery marched jauntily in the front middle & rear of the line, some of the

They seemed to feel that they were doing
a very noble thing and might
[illegible] ~~[illegible]~~
proudly march with an air of
~~[illegible]~~
triumph but
~~[illegible]~~ the instant the fellow

caught a glimpse of the English they darted
~~into the forest~~ so fast we caught
off ~~[illegible]~~
but a glance the red cap & soles of their
feet — The chief of the party alone
~~[illegible]~~
remained — he from being in front
had his hand by a Makololo
kindly grasped, ~~[illegible]~~
well known
* proved to be a slave of ~~[illegible]~~ [illegible]

Commandant of [illegible] own [illegible]
On asking him how he obtained these
captives he replied he had
While there ~~[illegible]~~
bought them — but on enquiring
of the people themselves — all . some
~~[illegible]~~ ~~[illegible]~~
four had been captured in war — While
this enquiry was going on he bolted to
kneel down and [illegible] clapped their hands
the captives

with great energy ~~struck in, hapless~~ They were thus left entirely on our hands and:
~~it became necessary for us to board~~ here, were

soon busy at work cutting the women

the advantage that it was more difficult

to cut the men adrift as each had his

neck in the ~~stout~~ gallant stick ~~six~~ on seven feet long,

long, kept in by an iron rod which was

riveted at both ends; ~~carefully there~~

with [illegible] a [illegible] lustily in the bishop's taffrail ~~and~~ one by one

the men were passed out into position

The women ~~and~~ on being told to take the ~~[illegible]~~ meal the, seemed to like

the natives in the Children ~~and the~~ mach

it as too good news to be true but

~~[illegible]~~ Sanda little bit

but after a little coaxing

went at with alacrity.

One of our men & the others had [illegible]

You cut off the things and tell us to eat

what sort of people are you?

~~[illegible]~~ where do you come from? The

Bishop was not present, having gone to

in a little stream below

bathe ~~[illegible]~~ the village ~~below~~

but on,

his return & warmly approved of all ~~he~~ had

been. He once had doubts but now

done ~~[illegible]~~ said he would have joined us

he

in the good work ~~if he~~ had been present

Eighty four, chiefly women & children

~~There~~ were ~~about~~ 84 liberated. And on

as all chose to stay and the Bishop kindly
attached them to his mission - ~~of the~~
~~[illegible]~~
to be educated as members of a
Christian family.
~~[illegible]~~, # / We proceeded
next morning to Soche ; , [illegible] one
liberated party, the Marchesses,
carrying the Bishop's goods; eight
others were paid as handsel [illegible]

carrying information to a raging party in front. Two of the Bishop's black men — from the Cape, Zealous Churchpeople having once been slaves themselves, volunteered to guard the premises during the night. ~~[illegible]~~

~~[illegible]~~

~~[illegible]~~

~~[illegible]~~ seizing the opportunity ~~and~~ we escaped and

~~[illegible]~~

~~[illegible]~~ one of the guard

~~[illegible]~~ Then

~~[illegible]~~ perceiving the loss rushed

out of the hole shouting "They're gone!

the prisoners are off!" And they were taken

rifle and the women were all skipping.
However, the slave traders being good enough
to get themselves off. Sixty were freed
next day in another village and cloth
enough to barter with them to clothe the
whole party better probably than they
had ever been before.

The portion of the highlands which the
Bishop wished to look at before deciding
on a settlement belonged to Chiwawa, the

we had met in our previous journey. On

reaching Magomero we heard that he

was dead and Chigunda the Chief instead

~~As soon as~~ Chigunda ~~learned that the~~

apparently of his own accord though possibly

Bishop intended to settle somewhere in

he may have learned that the

the Country ~~[illegible]~~

~~he~~ asked him to come and live with

them at Magomero saying there was room

enough for both. This hearty & spontaneous

invitation had considerable influence

expected his supplies to come up that
river but the Portuguese claiming it, must
had closed it as well as the Zambesi.
Our hopes were directed to the Rovuma
as a free highway into Lake Nyassa
and the vast interior: a steamer was
already ordered for the Lake and the Bishop
was more anxious to be near the Lake
and the Rovuma than the Shire.

223 ~~After~~ When the Bishop ~~concluded~~ decided to settle

a settlement, it was thought desirable

to prevent the country being depopulated

to [illegible] the Afghan Chiefs, [illegible]

Headman [illegible] to give up his [illegible],

and Kidnapps, [illegible] and [illegible] the

[illegible] of his people to peace & pursuits.

On ~~Monday~~ [illegible] the 22nd [illegible]

that the Afghans [illegible]

burning a village a few miles off

[illegible] the rescued [illegible], at the College

[illegible] an interview [illegible]

The mad exodus of Marguerite fleeing
from the war in front, the fugitives
had to leave all the food they possessed except
~~the small amount~~ the little they could carry
on their backs. They passed field
after field of Indian corn & beans
standing, ~~[illegible]~~ ripe for harvesting, but the
owners had been obliged to flee ~~away~~
~~leave them~~. The villages were
all deserted. One ~~[illegible]~~ which

[illegible] villages in flames [illegible] there heard a-

[illegible] and then the mingled with the

death wail of the Many [illegible] mourn

Mr. Bishop then engaged in prayer

-ing over the slain ~~God [illegible]~~,

~~[illegible]~~ rising from it we

~~[illegible]~~ saw a long line of Afghan [illegible]

[illegible] the [illegible] captives, wounded [illegible] the complete base of our party, we called

out that we had come to speak with

them but some of the Manganja who

followed us shouted "Our Chibisa" come

Chibisa being known as a

great conqueror & general

~~[illegible]~~ which the Ajawa ran off yelling &

We heard the words but they did

Ocean! Nkondo Nkondo war! war

not strike us at the moment

The captives threw down their loads

as neutralizing all our asser-

on the path and fled to the hills.

tions of peace

up from the village. And our prisoners,

they were all women as I remember,

[illegible] in proof that we had not

come to fight but to talk with them

The [illegible] heavy

as we remembered afterwards good

reason in many of our children

Flushed with the recent [illegible] over three villages, and

confident of an easy triumph [illegible]

three hundred of men they began to

shoot their poisoned arrows,

[illegible] them with great precision

one of our men was shot

a hundred yards through the arm [illegible]

[illegible]

up the ascent again, only

[illegible]

made them more eager to

to use the weapons which Providence

kill us – in the belief that my

[illegible]

retreat was evidence of fear –

closing up upon us

[illegible]

in bloodthirsty fury

The [illegible]

some

coming within fifty yards

[illegible]

dancing hideously – others

had quit, surrounded us

availing themselves of the [illegible] long

awaiting [illegible] hard by

grass [illegible] foliage

others made off with

[illegible] of their

their –

women [illegible] a large body of slaves

22 X drove them off and on seeing

the range of the rifles ~~[illegible]~~

they very soon desisted

finally drove them off ~~it~~ the village

was ~~[illegible]~~ a mile [illegible] [illegible]

was [illegible] ~~it~~ with all the body, [illegible]

We ~~[illegible]~~ [illegible] [illegible] [illegible]

Carefully [illegible] shouted [illegible] the warriors

on the hill, that they would follow

and kill us when we slept.

We Returned to the village

~~It was past [illegible] at night before~~

~~we got back to~~

~~we~~ reached ~~the village~~ [illegible] the

morning, after a hungry fatigue, and

most unpleasant day ~~and the~~

~~[illegible]~~

Next morning the Bishop proposed that we should go after the Ajawa to rescue the captive Manganja in their hands and also drive these man-stealing marauders out of the country. The religious were warmly in favour of this except Dr Livingstone who said no, better wait and see the effect of what we have already done; it might be enough; he would come up and see if anything more was necessary after having to learn from the Bishop

The old Chief Chinama he came over ~~to see us~~ ~~he was~~ glad to see his friends again, and glad that we had built, of the Ajawa who had fled to "Zomba" he insisted on the Bishop's coming to live with him, Chigunda was a child of his, the Bishop should live with the father and not remain with the child And he, evident that the old chief-man, wanted the Bishop to protect

mortality was declared "Then I'm killed" he remarked "I'm ~~already~~ dead already". He was reminded of the fact that he and the other Manganja chiefs had encouraged the Ajawa slave traders to come among them in former years and by selling their people for cloth they fostered this slave trade which was now desolating the land. The Ajawa had ~~[illegible]~~ that there was a famine among the Manganja

chiefs, all were jealous of each other and
glad when any calamity befel their neighbours
and they concluded that it would be more
profitable to capture the slaves than
to purchase them.

A stockade was placed across the
entrance to the Mission station,

fairly established in his new quarters, and leaving a Quarter Master behind him we returned to the ship to prep.

cloth a piece per day. This

~~the~~ [Every] Woman's great wages ~~were then~~

~~was so difficulty in obtaining them~~

~~to~~ more than twice the sum [required] to pay

~~were eager to hire them~~ [eagerly] ... eagerly offe

their services. The ~~only~~ [chief] difficulty

crowd of fellows in and ~~we had taken~~
had we not taken
down the names ~~of those who took a~~
to guide us in
in the morning ~~in which to~~ passing ~~them~~
up
in the way ~~[illegible] those who~~
claims would have made by those
who took hold during the last 10 minutes
of the ~~flag~~ pouring ~~as [illegible] did~~
~~on the first day~~. The men you
village [illegible] it to the [illegible] and
all we had to do was to say to the
[illegible] that we want to [illegible]

were passed, the largest of which was

the Mathuru Madse and the ~~Kisung~~ Lesung we

The inhabitants of both banks are

remarkably civil and obliging

and possessing a tool and courage

some of every independent of their ruins

having probably developed their more

There is often a surprising contrast between villages neighbours,

amicable feelings. ~~Some~~ of the

one is well off and thriving, having good huts, plenty of [illegible]

~~[illegible]~~ ~~[illegible] to be well~~ off having

cows & native cloth around, people are free & generous &

good [illegible] tilled crops to sell [illegible],
plenty of food ~~the~~ ~~native~~ clothing, which
in the head [illegible]
~~them~~ the inhabitants, many old houses
distilling, suspicious, withal rather, for sale
ill fed ~~and~~ decently clad, though
the land [illegible] there well [illegible] as
fertile as that of their neighbours,
We followed the river for the most
part to avoid ascending the stiff
reaches but on comparatively smooth
path farther inland, over which a
road could easily be made.
Some of the cataracts are very fine
of ~~Latitude~~
the river falling 1200 ft in 35 miles,
many [illegible] cataracts

and deep waters of the upper Shire
and proceeded up the river accompanied
by the land party on the right bank
There is but little current on the
upper Shire and this part of the
river may almost be regarded as
a prolongation of Lake Nyassa
though one day a gale blew
Seldom does the current exceed
one knot an hour while that of

The women of Manganja fugitives, been living in temporary huts on the right bank having recently been driven from their villages on the other side by the Ajawa. Some were busy cultivating the ground and planting the little corn they had brought with them, and the effects of hunger were already visible on those whose food

tried hard to have us go on Andra

off the Ajana. This is the second

much back along the same ...

occupying the same important post

the other day, the same ministry

a Balinjee ... in the Summerse

flow out of Nyassa are covered with

~~thousands~~ hundreds of elephants by day.

Owing to Cape Maclear being far to the south of

on the left bank of the Shire, we continued on the same side and

of keeping ~~we~~ kept to the west land party,

on the west side of the Lake and

saw upwards of two hundred miles

of its length and would have seen

it all but unluckily we have food became

human skeletons and a few stones,
together which, generally disappear as soon as they
leave us. [illegible]
and the [illegible] is [illegible]
Miles in breadth, but [illegible]
[illegible] goes [illegible]

great body, of Nyassa,

it not far from where he turned

back came about a mile from the

[illegible] the [illegible] [illegible] follow

we were on the lake in perhaps the
stormiest season of the year (Sept. Oct.)
and were repeatedly detained by the
gales. At times, while sailing
pleasantly over the blue water, with
a gentle breeze, suddenly, and
without any warning we heard

in one of these gales and anchored
in seven fathoms a mile from shore
with the sea breaking, around & beyond us.
The waves & mist dashes rushed
upon us in threes with a few minutes
of comparative quiet between the
successive charges. Had one of these
white-crested masses broken over our
frail bark nothing could have saved us

set the horns to face those ~~strangers~~
constellations. Any one of which might
be carrying our fate in its heavy heart.
A lone dark detached, oddly shaped cloud came
steadily from the mountains and hung
for hours directly over our heads. Our black crew
became haunted and unable to sit up

Swallow up the boat. They're lost!

They're all dead! when at last we got ashore they saluted us warmly as after a long absence. Like [illegible]

received no great [illegible] from the

weel; the 3 times we observed we

passing, this part appear to be [illegible],

in as much water as the Shire was

carrying out. Distinct line-

-marks on the rocks show that for

some time during the rainy season

the water of the Lake is three feet

above the point to which it falls, towards

other streams from the mountains

in front when swollen by the rains

may be sufficient to account for

the rise in the Lake without ~~the~~ any

large river in the North ~~which some~~

the natives ~~speaking of that which~~

The existence of any large river
nearest the North end denied
though to us it seemed necessary to
account for the lines of pumice

the west side of the Lake with the
~~flow~~

bays of nearly similar form each
having ~~an~~ open sandy beach and pebbly shores
~~being~~ separated from the neighbouring by
a rocky headland ~~with~~ detached
rocks extending some distance out to
sea. The great southwestern bay is
a very good harbour, the only really
good one we saw on the west side.
The land adjacent to the lakes is level
fertile and in some places marshy
with millions of ducks, geese, loons, cranes &

other grains, roots &c &c

Ten or a dozen miles, ~~back of the~~ behind the rich plains are high ranges of well wooded hills, running nearly parallel with the Lake Shore presenting, in many points the magnificent views of range towering behind range, highest still higher until the distant lofty mountains bound the prospect by rearing ~~peaks~~ their summits ~~against~~ to the sky.

Towards the North the plain becomes narrower until near where we turned it disappears altogether and the mountains

rise abruptly out of the lake forming

the east boundary of which we describe

as an extend in table land well

suited for pasturage and agriculture and

only partially
occupied at present by the tribe of Zulus

who came from the south within the remembrance of 50 years

ago and own large herds of cattle.

Never before in Africa have we seen

anything like the dense population

Lake Nyassa. In the southern parts

standing gazing at the novel sight of a boat under sail, and whenever we landed we were surrounded, in a few seconds by hundreds of men, women and children who had hastened to have a stare at the ~~strange~~ wild animals.

To see the animals feed was the great attraction; never did Zoological Society's lions draw a bigger, such multitudes. The crowds round us looking on apparently with the deeper

but they goodnaturedly

interest; ~~the [illegible]~~

kept each other ~~to~~ a line made on

~~[illegible]~~

~~the~~ sand which left us room

~~[illegible]~~

~~to~~ dine

~~The aroma of black humanity~~

~~perspiring is not pleasant while~~

~~one is eating.~~

They cultivate the soil pretty extensively

fariña constitutes the main support of the inhabitants. During a portion of the year the northern dwellers on the earth have a curious harvest which furnishes a singular sort of food. As we approached our northern limit great clouds as of smoke rise, from tracts of burning grass were observed away in a S. Easterly direction

morning we started through one of the clouds on our own side and found on the hot way, and found that countless millions of midges. They filled the air in immense layers and covered the water. Eyes and mouth had to be kept closed while passing through this living cloud, they struck

people gather these minute insects and bake them with a little [illegible] into thick cakes, millions of midges in a cake. A midge cake an inch thick and as large as the blue bonnet of a ploughman was brought to us; it was very dark in colour and tasted not unlike the [illegible] red herring. Abundance of ~~[illegible]~~ excellent fish are found running up the river to spawn like our salmon at home. The largest are over two feet in length, [illegible] the best we have ever eaten in Africa. They were going up the river in Augt and Sept and furnish [illegible] profitable employment to many fishermen. ~~Dams~~ Weirs were constructed

single entrance the Sanjika ~~[illegible]~~
has small chance of escape
~~[illegible]~~
~~[illegible]~~" for ~~and~~ a third distance
below nets are ~~stretched~~ across from bank
to bank so that it seemed a marvel
how even the most sagacious Sanji'ka
could get up without being taken
unless a free passage up the rivers
left at night. On the 22nd
~~of July the following year whilst we~~
~~were waiting at the bay we found~~
~~a native catching fish with poison~~

at the [illegible] mouth of the Zambesi, and among the fish taken were two fine Sanjika. Is it possible for them to run up through the cataracts?

The lake fish are caught chiefly in nets though men and even women with babies on their backs are occa-

quinine. In deep water some
kinds are taken by lowering to a great
depth the fish baskets which are attached
by a long cord to a float around
which is often tied a mass of grass
or weeds. As are all very cheaply made traps
for the deep sea fish. Fleet 9

been running, Our Makololo acted
bold in handling canoes, the Batoka
men could beat them as they were
unwilling to cross the Zambesi when
the wind blew fresh,

-pression to the disease and we found
that the two forenoon sleepers, have
been heard about with the greater part
of the night. In the afternoon they
began to bestir themselves; examin-

fellows are lurking in the water day

their nets. Though there are many
crocodiles
~~Alligators~~ in the Lake and some of

extraordinary size the fishermen say

that it is a rare thing for any one to

be carried off by these reptiles ~~It~~

~~And it would appear that the alligators~~
When the crocodile
Can easily obtain abundance of fish
^ their natural food

~~as~~ they seldom attack men ~~[illegible]~~
^ But when unable to see to catch their

~~the case~~ Many [illegible]
prey by reason of the muddiness of the
water in floods they are very dangerous.

cloth woven in many of the southern
villages, it is evident that a goodly
number of busy hands and patient
heads must be employed in the cotton

manufacture of cloth from the mul-
berry tree is ever going on from
one end of the Lake to the other
and both toil and time are required
to prepare the bark and put it
through the various ~~steps~~ processes which
render it soft and fit to wear

women are frightfully ugly and
really make themselves hideous
by the ~~[illegible]~~ means they adopt with
the view of rendering their persons
beautiful and attractive.

The pelele or ornament for the
upper lip is universally worn by the
ladies, the most valuable being

two of one firm and Price, painted

candles thrust through the lip, and

projecting beyond the tip of the nose;

a few are the ... of a ...

~~a~~ kind of pipe bead ornament in

~~stone~~ ~~And all a little ... the~~

fashion — "sweet things" in

~~..., looks as if the ... just came~~

their way

~~... and ... in a ... domestic~~

~~squabble~~, All are tattooed ...

269 raise up little knobs on the skin of
Some ~~[illegible]~~ their faces, after a fashion
~~That~~ makes them look as if
~~[illegible]~~ covered
all over with ~~[illegible]~~ ugly, warts, or pimples
~~[illegible]~~
~~[illegible]~~ k. The
young girls are ~~[illegible]~~ pretty, good looking
before ~~[illegible]~~ the ages advance to
harden the features & give
~~[illegible]~~
them the appearance of age
~~[illegible]~~
~~[illegible]~~ in character. The

men are of them while a good many

~~[illegible]~~ as we ~~they~~ put it Middle, ~~[illegible]~~

"we're better than they should be",

went near as ~~often happen~~

If [illegible] ~~as happened [illegible]~~ as we often did to see the fish

when a net was drawn a fish was

always ~~[illegible]~~ offered. So long [illegible]

past a number of such we had

just dragged the net ashore at

one of the fine fisheries in the upper

Shire [illegible] harbor and water

village on the Lake, a number of the natives manned two canoes, took out their seine and dragged it and made us a present of the entire haul; they had had done this for us. The Mathaij Chief Marigo was ~~remarkably~~ specially generous and gave bountiful present of food and beer. "Do they ever such things in your country," he asked, pointing to ~~the~~ his arm back to shoulder with copper [illegible] also [illegible], The [illegible]

Chung Mangkonbera also treats us

with kindness; but ~~they are also~~

~~[illegible]~~ at ~~[illegible]~~ the same trade ~~[illegible]~~, [illegible]

they are dishonest & uncivil. To

that trade becomes a flight [illegible] a chase

[illegible]

~~[illegible]~~ [illegible] go[illegible]. The

first question at these fake [illegible] places

as well as food. ~~There are a great~~

~~[illegible]~~ much of foreign cloth, beads

and brass wire are worn by the people

all these coming, and some have

muskets; The slave trade here

is going on just now at a fearful

rate. Two enterprising Arabs have

built a dow on the Lake and are

town of Ibo and doubles supplies the

vile market. One of our Cruisers

called there the first years and

was taken it first of the largest slaver

expected at the time; The slaves

1900 appears exclusion of the export

to the Portuguese slave trading towns

of small arms & gunpowder on the Lake

commencing, cut the neck of this

infamous traffic as all must cross

the Lake or the upper Shire.

Prob 1900 appears ~~[illegible]~~ necessary, comprising all

the suppression of the slave trade.

Then we'll all climb up the stairs,
to die of slow starvation among the rocks
and on the hills?

A little way south of
~~Not far from where~~ the Arab's trading
station the first robbery was
~~[illegible]~~

277 suffered in Africa occurred

~~people of Nyassa are as far advanced~~

and ~~we~~ learned that the Nyassa people

~~a little~~ ~~more~~ [illegible] civilized than [illegible]

~~We~~ have a [illegible] thieves among them.

Never except when we suspected danger or treachery did we set a watch

~~[illegible]~~

and when at last

One of this [illegible] ~~[illegible]~~

between 3 & 4 o'clock in ~~[illegible]~~

called [illegible] the morning, ~~[illegible]~~

had a touch of

~~[illegible]~~ fever, ~~[illegible]~~

~~[illegible]~~

we were quietly

~~[illegible]~~ rifles ~~[illegible]~~

relieved

~~[illegible]~~ of [illegible] goods while ~~[illegible]~~

the owners rifles & Revolvers always

[illegible] ~~[illegible]~~

awaking as

~~performance [illegible]~~ ~~[illegible]~~

~~[illegible] became apparent~~

The loss of one victim was announced by "My bag is gone" ~~[illegible]~~

~~[illegible]~~ with all my clothes and my tools too." "Both of mine are off" he responded [illegible], and mine too chimes in the third [illegible] with the bag of [illegible] all the [illegible]!"

Is the cloth taken? was the eager enquiry, as that would have been equivalent to all our money [illegible]

It was taken and [illegible] secured

~~[illegible]~~

By the sort of honour said to be among thieves, those rogues ~~[illegible]~~

the [illegible] became [illegible] part of
[illegible] ~~[illegible]~~ possibly thinking that they might
be of use to any ~~[illegible]~~ or at least of no use to them,
They carried off specimens we had collected
~~and~~ from our notes, [illegible] all
our clothing leaving [illegible] of us [illegible]
with nothing but what he happened
(Leave 4 lines here)
to have on at the time; Thinking
~~[illegible] that the [illegible]~~ helpless
~~[illegible] the [illegible] left [illegible]~~
our rifles [illegible] being left [illegible] with

humiliating to be so thoroughly, ~~done part,~~ fleeced by a few black rascals. ~~We couldn't keep back the right account of and one those couldn't keep another We have been robbed before in that~~

A few of the best fisheries appear to be private property. We found shells from a stone or common

to purchase some but they refused that "The pork did not belong to them, they would send for the proprietor of the place and he would sell to us.

The gentleman arrived in a short time and readily sold what we wanted.

Some of their buryin[g] grounds are wonderfully well arranged and

its wide spreading branches throw their kindly shade over the last resting place of the dead. Several other magnificent trees grow around the hallowed spot. The graves were raised as they are at this time but all lay north and south, the heads appearing,

had used in their daily employments,
whilst amidst the piles of
a piece of a fishing net and a broken
paddle told us that a fisherman
slept beneath that roof. The graves
of the women had the mortar and
the heavy ~~stick~~ pestle used in pounding the
corn and the basket in which the

of several of the years. The people

of the neighbouring villages were friendly,

and obliging, and willingly brought out

food for sale,

The northern part of the Tk. was

the abode of anarchy, and bloodshed

The Mazithe live in the hills and

make sudden swoops on the defenceless

(Leave 3 lines)

villages of the plains. All the)

their attacks upon [illegible] Manganja. The thickets around their villages, enabled them formerly to keep off the Mazitu who were afraid to venture where they could not use their shields. Beyond, Many hundreds in their burned villages and the dead bodies of many who had fallen by the Mazitu spear but a few days when fear fell upon them on the South

Dr [illegible] both the [illegible]
directed the boat to call for him in a bay in sight and
both the parties proceeded (North, In and

from the land party, struck inland

on approaching the foot of the mountain

which rises abruptly out of the lake

Supposing that they had heard of a path

around the [illegible] the boat held

on her course but [illegible] began to blow ~~[illegible]~~
a gale so that
~~them~~ [illegible] she had to [illegible]

the land party, but they could see

nothing of them, and we decided as soon

as it was safe to put to sea, thinking

they would rejoin the Lake in port
('Leave 5 lines here)
We passed in a short time an island

mass of rocks on which was a number

of armed natives with some young

women apparently living there. The

head man told us that he had been

by night to kill and plunder,

They said there was a path behind

the hills and we sailed on,

A few Miles above we came upon

another
a still larger band of pirates and

gathering predators kept on for some
time after all the others gave up the
chase. 'A good large [illegible] [illegible] a [illegible]–
the boat headed away for them

then another gale compelled us to seek
shelter in a bay. Here we found
a number of wretched fugitives from
the slave trade on the opposite shore
of the Lake. The original inhabitants
having been swept off the year before
by the Mazitu. In the deserted

range apparently aspiring to be near the
with trees. We tried to purchase
food but they had nothing but a little
dried Manioc (root) and a few fish
They asked 2 yards of cloth for the handful
a ~~[illegible]~~ only of fish. On the way the Ron
former prisoners tried to leave us, scared by
cutting out that they had lots of ivory to
sell. Owing to ~~storms~~ a ~~continuance~~ succession of heavy ~~storms~~ gales
it was the fourth day before we found

had been hired

having ~~been~~ ~~turned~~ out, after pro-ceeding a short distance on the path we heard from them [illegible] that they would like to stay several days before the [illegible] join the [illegible] again, and consequently [illegible] but the boat was way out of sight when they reached the Coast [illegible] mountainside [illegible] then tired but proved [illegible] the [illegible] to be [illegible] fully [illegible] [illegible] the [illegible] all the [illegible] with more than ~~[illegible]~~ five miles,

A small party, of armed Mazites appe
suddenly the 1 day, and in the mean time
was shouted to people on the side
flight. On seeing that the man did
run away, they sat down under a tree
They called out, as the Dr was walking up
to them Stop! don't come here! &t

Cared but spare one as that regards

the food he had, They then went
(Scarce 5 lines)
off. The [illegible] general Marker

from [illegible] to the land party, the

Commune, called Snuffie, a chief [illegible]

[illegible], afraid of the Magistrate

and bitter the [illegible] [illegible]

up that day, and could [illegible] the

the [illegible] of the Magistrates making them

uncommonly lame. The Deserters

all back to Matavai [illegible] but two

came along to the ship and was

on looking in one of the canoes which

had belonged to the [illegible] of [illegible]

the [illegible]

[illegible] when we met him.

Then he overtook us to the guardships
of his comrades who ran back to
their encampment. They were
all exhausted for joy and fired off their
muskets. He had heard from his

gave him good tea and him was
he had promised us but a foot of land
fellows between Allan Kumbein and
illumigo seized him as a slave, slipp
him and put a slave stick on his
neck and we all about the well hunk

a fathom of dark cloth

Elephants are numerous on the borders of the Lake and frequently leave their spoor near the villages. Hippopotamus in the creeks & lagoons and Lions are sometimes seen near the Lake. Some of each were shot for food during our journey

a single tusk apiece and were each killed by a single shot. It is [illegible] a hunger as a beast which depends, for food on the rifle and most generally the game except when game is as abundant as it is on the Zambesi in the interior,

I've shot one morning, on this trip two hippo and an elephant perhaps a dozen tons of meat in all and two days after that we had only the last

quietly, flapping the gypsies he can

Glad of the opportunity of getting

some fresh meat he soon landed

and fired into one. They all

retreated into a marsh, full of

game in the way between the village,

Our men gave chase and fired

into the herd as they came up with

an attempt to charge, Harry bowled this legs with a rifle bullet to prevent his escape a [illegible], he fired into him at 40 yds range

he fell. One whale-fisher from the North of Ireland, a most [illegible] useful man, happened to fire the last shot, and as soon as he saw the animal fall he turned to the [illegible] glimpse to the [illegible] exclaimed "It was *me*, shot that done it, Sir."
In a few minutes afterwards a

wanted for ourselves the remainder was
given to the natives to take the meat.
They rushed at it then like hungry
hyenas, and in a wonderfully short
time every inch of it was taken up.
The tusks weigh 62 lbs apiece.
A large number of ivory might easily
be obtained from the people of Nyassa.
We were frequently told of them having
it in their huts.

of the Karonde we were overtaken by a number

of [illegible] traders, the chief Arab who had

been settled for ~~three~~ 12 years as a trader

at Katanga to the south of Cazembe

~~[illegible] Cazembe~~'s country. They had

just brought down ivory, malachite

copper rings and slaves to exchange

for cloth. The malachite was dug

out of the ground where they lived. They

knew Lake Tanganyika well but had

not heard of the [illegible] lake slip. The

power of their large establishment of living,

that the Arab must be chary of any-
his following, can never form a [illegible]
[illegible]
trade." It is difficult to get at [illegible]
out of the natives
or draw any reliable information respecting
the country in point. Some are suspicious
of travellers, ~~and~~ those at times contradict
in their answers, and are unwilling to
commit themselves to any particulars,
while others draw largely upon their
imagination, and talk of ~~giant~~ ~~[illegible]~~ men
in their
wells, answers ~~[illegible]~~ equal to the
most wonderful tales of ancient
they say what
travellers, or ~~[illegible]~~ they think

end of the table we enquired of an inhabitant

looking in search of the South pole. "The

other end of the table!" he exclaimed

in real or well feigned astonishment

who ever heard of such a thing — Why

if a ~~man~~ one started when a mere boy

to walk to the other end of the table

he would be an old grey headed man

before he got there. We had never

Said only [illegible] into the Moravia

But above that their testimony differs

One saying that it flows past the Lake

but not only [illegible] and others equally

positive that it is several days journey

from the Lake [illegible]. So with the

river reported as flowing into the Lake

from the north. Village after village

in [illegible] 12 [illegible] of a large river which

sea in its existence altogether, for
at the same time the names of the
different localities, places round the head
of the Lake., At a village we
slept at near the fort there we were
told that a very large party with
three canoes had just crossed the

guns in the evening and people [illegible]
the report that they must be at least 6
hours away. In descending the Shire
we found concealed among the road
belt of Papyrus which is called
Tamalombe
just where the river expands a
number of Manganja fugitives
who had been driven from their homes
by the Ajawa raid, So [illegible]
[illegible] the Papyrus [illegible]

no one passing by on the shore would
even dream that human beings
lived there. They came hither from
~~belong~~ the south by means of their canoes, which
also enabled them to obtain a living
from the fine fish which abound
in the lakelet. They had large
quantities of salt [illegible] [illegible] upon bark

as we please them & [illegible] dare not interfere,

Merchants complain that they could not get men to go into the interior to trade — they are all [illegible] in the country. Many places [illegible] [illegible] near the Lucabo" [illegible] [illegible] for [illegible]

A [illegible] in town Calvia, off a Cargo. The Portuguese [illegible] with the Govt. for allowing us to come into the country, secondly evident from their remarks that the Comings, check the slave trade and they say all [illegible] in the [illegible] of the slaves,

Mission might do as the Portuguese [illegible]. Raise their own rice, wheat, potatoes, pigs, sheep, cattle, [illegible] the [illegible] [illegible]

a piece of bread & meal [illegible] shares [illegible] the [illegible] though [illegible] better
each [illegible] lighting and [illegible]

On seeing the desolation caused by the slave trade [illegible]

Remarks of Jack's observation a very [illegible] ~~[illegible]~~ [illegible] [illegible] ~~[illegible]~~ [illegible]

Jolly Bill if the devil don't catch those fellows we might as well have no devil at all; said in bottling brandy

Bury the [illegible] [illegible] [illegible] [illegible] a headman the [illegible] [illegible] [illegible] [illegible] strangers

Chinsamba's reply to the Ajawa This is our Lake, why do you send ~~[illegible]~~ white men to look at it. These men came here, stole nothing Killed no one, paid for all they got, walked over and looked at the Lake and ~~[illegible]~~ ~~all they got~~ and then went away and that is all we Know about them petty jealousy

A woman holds her pelele & [illegible] places her hand over her mouth as [illegible] [illegible] to [illegible] [illegible].

Parting [illegible] [illegible] [illegible] them,

Dr [illegible] [illegible] ~~[illegible]~~ escaped fever on [illegible] [illegible]

Plants medicinal & for food. names of [illegible] [illegible]
& herbs best for cattle, We come to teach these people but what can we teach them? they [illegible] [illegible]
[illegible] [illegible]
Though the ivory trade

has nearly stopped in consequence of the high price & scarcity of cotton cloth, yet the new phase of the slave trade [illegible], women into the interior to [illegible] for ivory is carrying it on in [illegible] the [illegible]

However was [illegible] ship built / was it on the land? [illegible] & on the [illegible] how did the [illegible] get [illegible] & [illegible] [illegible] [illegible] was built in the water

No permanency to their villages at present from [illegible] slaving and when a favourite chief dies the village is deserted and they move off to a new site. [illegible] [illegible] on the [illegible] cloth [illegible] p 89

www.ingramcontent.com/pod-product-compliance
Lightning Source LLC
Chambersburg PA
CBHW030811230426
43667CB00008B/1163
9783743606401